Preparing Your Family to Manage Wealth

A comprehensive guide to estate and succession planning,
and to building a family team

Roy O. Williams

MONTEREY PACIFIC INSTITUTE ❖ MARINA, CA

Copyright © 1992 by Roy O. Williams

All rights reserved.

This book is sold with the understanding that the subject matter covered herein is of a general nature and does not constitute legal, accounting or other professional advice for any specific individual or situation. Anyone planning to take action in any of the areas that this book describes should, of course, seek professional advice from accountants, lawyers, tax, and other advisers, as would be prudent and advisable under their given circumstances.

Monterey Pacific Institute
P.O. Box 829, Marina, CA 93933

Book Design and Typesetting by Diane Parker

Library of Congress Card Catalog Number: 91-67455

ISBN 1-880710-00-5

Dedication

I would like to dedicate this book to my wife, Diana, to our three sons, Scott, Eric and Dan, and to their wives and children. They are the ones who taught me the most about being in balance—as a father, husband and businessman. Thank you for being you, and for contributing so much to my life. I love you.

This book is also dedicated to the loving memory of a dear friend who exemplified balance, love and harmony in his life and family—Ed Stanley.

Acknowledgments

Four years ago when I started writing this book, I thought it would be easy to dictate my thoughts, organize them and compile the book from ideas and tools for helping clients and their families. Little did I know how much help I would need, and how much I would receive. So the following acknowledgements are to honor those who were so helpful to me in completing this book.

First I want to thank all of our clients from the last twenty-seven years. You and your families were the ones who trusted us and went along with what must have appeared at times to be strange ideas. Your homes and offices were the classrooms where we learned ways to work, play, laugh and love together. They were where we learned how to build trust, and how to explore and share our ideas in a safe environment. Without all of you, this company would not exist and this book could never have been written.

My thanks to Fernando Flores, Philip Hallstein and all of those at Business Design Associates for their insight and coaching on the art of listening and building trust. I'm grateful to Ed Stanley for his sage advice and the analogy of taking the training wheels off the kids' bikes at some age—whether five or sixty; to Dean Edward C. Halbach, Jr., of the Boalt Hall School of Law, University of California, Berkeley, for his wisdom, judgment, objectivity and friendship. Thanks also to Theo Wells and Nori Huddle, both of whom spent many hours helping me dictate by asking good questions and challenging the clarity of my thoughts.

I especially want to thank the friends and clients who went through all the drafts of the book, and gave me many suggestions on better ways to communicate the points we were trying to make. They are:

- ❖ Art and Sarah Ludwick, Rain Bird Manufacturing Co.
- ❖ Bob and Wendy Graham, Katalysis Foundation, San Tomo Foods
- ❖ Budge and Arlene Brown, Brown Enterprises
- ❖ Kelin Gersick, Professor, California School of Professional Psychology, and partner in Owner Managed Business Institute, Santa Barbara, California
- ❖ Joanie Bronfman, social psychologist and specialist in inherited wealth
- ❖ John Levy, specialist in inherited wealth
- ❖ Jordan Paul, psychologist and author
- ❖ Ginger Taylor, Client Coordinator and promise keeper, The Williams Group
- ❖ Gordon Snyder, President, The Williams Group
- ❖ Maria Teresa Caen, literary agent
- ❖ Cindy Ridgeway, my able assistant.
- ❖ John O'Neil, President, California School of Professional Psychology, San Francisco, California
- ❖ Paul Booth, Inheritors Coach, The Williams Group
- ❖ Alberta Moran, Client Service Manager, The Williams Group
- ❖ John Brady, President, Growth Technologies, Inc.
- ❖ Geoffrey S. Way, attorney at law

A special thank you to Colin Ingram, my collaborator, and the one person without whom this book would not have been written. Thank you, Colin, for your energy and sage advice.

And to everyone who helped me: Thank you all.

Contents

Author's Comments

This book is based on my twenty-seven years experience in dealing with special kinds of entrepreneurs—those who have been very successful and have built up substantial wealth. While there are increasing numbers of successful female entrepreneurs and those with non-traditional families, most successful entrepreneurs are still mature males with a wife, grown-up children and, usually, grandchildren. While the information I have presented applies equally to non-traditional situations, I have found it convenient to frequently refer to the family entrepreneur as male, to the spouse as female and to the family as a traditional one with a husband, wife and children. I hope the reader will understand that the information presented is for both genders and for all types of families.

A second point of usage in this book are the terms "children" and "kids." In many cases, the beings that parents give birth to and raise are still referred to as children even after they are fully grown. At age 83, my mother still calls me one of her children. Although this is understandable, what are the implications for our adult offspring? Is this a box we put them in so that they never really grow up in our minds, and we behave accordingly?

Two of our clients are twin brothers, each aged 65, who have three grown-up sons between them. The three sons, who are all in their mid-thirties, work in the family business and have always been called "the boys." Even the receptionist referred to them as "the boys." Just changing the pattern and calling them by their names changed the image of "the boys" in the office almost immediately and enhanced their credibility and performance. So when we as parents and grandparents refer to our adult offspring as "children," we should take care that we are not creating the wrong image in the minds of ourselves or others.

In this book I have tried to be sensitive to this problem. Nevertheless, the nature of the English language requires that the term be used in some cases. So I ask the reader's indulgence, when I refer to the grown-up offspring of entrepreneurs as their "children," and hope you will accept this usage with good grace.

Much of the information in this book also applies to families without entrepreneurs; those that have inherited or built-up family wealth through means other than an active family business. Management of family wealth is similar in many ways to the management of a business. It requires skills in dealing with people, delegating authority and achieving a high level of knowledge and expertise. It also involves considerable time. In effect, the management of family wealth is, itself, a family business. In this book, wherever I have referred to the family business, I specifically intend for the information to apply to the management of family wealth as well.

For various reasons, the majority of my clients have been persons of substantial net worth. Accordingly, the examples used throughout this book for amounts of income, investment, recreation, etc., represent those amounts that I have typically encountered. However, the family problems that I describe in this book, as well as their solutions, are also applicable to families with smaller assets, and readers should not be dissuaded because they are not (yet) millionaires.

With the exception of a few instances where I have stated otherwise, the names of my clients who are mentioned in this book, their types of businesses and their locations have been changed in order to maintain confidentiality. Some of the circumstances and events I have described have been altered or simplified to clarify the point I want to make. Otherwise, the many persons I have portrayed in this book are based on real families in real situations.

Introduction

In my travels around the world over the years, I have listened to the grown-up children of affluent parents and grandparents tell about themselves and their families. Here are some quotes from these children:

"I hate my dad for weighing me down with financial burdens I never asked for."

"I am embarrassed and ashamed of my family's wealth."

"My brothers and I are always fighting over money."

"My father only loves with money. He sends presents but he never shows up."

"If you are rich it doesn't matter whether or not you are honest or courteous or kind."

"All the things I believe and trust came from my nanny. I don't know who my parents really are."

"Money determines who you are—nothing else really matters."

"I buy my clothes at thrift stores to make sure I look like everyone else."

"Money is a vulgar topic and should not be discussed."

I could go on for pages with comments reflecting poor self-image, despair, anger, hatred, embarrassment, abandonment and need for love among the young and the grown-up children of wealthy families. What has caused such family discord and skewed values?

As an example, I recently spent some time with a father who kept telling me how many excellent deals he had recently made. From the tone of the conversation, I felt that this man had lost sight of what was really important, so I asked him a series of blunt questions. I asked him how much time he spent with his teenaged children. Did he ever spend time with them just simply listening? Was he satisfied with the role model he had created for them? Was he more concerned with his children acquiring values based on integrity or on values centered around making money? And lastly, if his children were important to him, could he justify the amount of time he spent away from his family? His answers reflected the fact that this entrepreneur had done nothing to prepare his children to live wisely. For him, the acquisition of wealth has been accomplished but at the tremendous cost of lack of communication, trust and knowing who his children are.

The number of families with potential problems of this kind is increasing. According to a recent survey by the Federal Reserve, more than 1.7 million households in the United States have more than a million dollars in wealth, and projections show that this is going to increase dramatically. What kind of adults will spring from these affluent families, and will they have the values and judgment and maturity to use their wealth wisely?

If a business is part of the inherited package, all the problems of affluence are compounded. From the founder of a business to the third generation, only fifteen out of a hundred businesses survive, and stories abound of inheritors who have ruined the family business and wasted their lives in the process.

In family after family I have worked with, I have witnessed anguish and bitterness—children growing up with poor values; communication within the family nonexistent; entrepreneur fathers or mothers estranged from their grown-up children; and family members harboring bitterness that twists and shapes their lives.

Few books or courses of instruction have been available for parents who want to raise mature, balanced children who will be able to receive and responsibly use money that they have inherited. This issue badly needs to be addressed. In my own practice I have seen heirs battling over succession issues to the point where they spent some twenty million dollars in legal fees. I've watched families tear themselves apart over perceived unfairness in their inheritance. And I've seen vital, wealth-producing businesses, built up over a lifetime of effort, destroyed out of ignorance and lack of preparation.

This book fills the gap for the generational transfer of wealth and knowledge. It tells you how to give your children—whether they are young or adults—the information and experience to use wealth effectively. The processes I describe in this book are not theories—they are based on my actual experiences working with families for over two-and-one half decades. These processes are not quick fixes; ingrained family attitudes take time to change. But as you invest your time, energy and heart into them, they will yield many benefits. Your spouse and your grown-up children will be prepared to inherit your wealth and use it wisely. You will be able to build a financial safety net for your heirs which will provide income through several generations. Most importantly, with these processes, you will empower your family to take control of the succession; you will help them to deal confidently with authority figures; and your family will become a real working team, where decisions are based on sound information, trust and mutual respect.

A successful transfer of wealth to your succeeding generations means more than money. It means raising children who are strong enough to test and confirm your values in their own life experiences, and who will become competent, self-confident, generous and loving persons in their own right. And finally, the successful transfer of your values, as well as your wealth, means that the very best part of you will survive to benefit the lives of all your succeeding generations. You could not leave a greater legacy.

As you begin working with your family to manage wealth, you will be involved with several processes you haven't used before. As such, you will be a beginner, and beginners can become impatient, frustrated and exasperated with the pace of their progress. I personally received a meaningful lesson on "beginning" which I'd like to share with you, hoping it will help you as much as it did me.

As part of a course exercise for company managers, each of us in the group was given three silk scarves and asked to juggle them. Of course, we were not particularly interested in scarf juggling but we were asked to go along with it. After about ten minutes of dropping the scarves on the floor and picking them up, I decided it was a pointless exercise—a waste of time, so I stopped. My instructor asked me if I felt as exasperated as I looked. I told him, yes, that I didn't see the point of my standing there, throwing scarves into the air and picking them up again.

He then asked me if I was a master juggler, a journeyman juggler or even a minimally competent juggler, to which I responded, no. He asked if I was a beginner, and I said yes. In view of that, he said, shouldn't I expect lots of scarves to be on the floor? And he suggested that perhaps the cause of my frustration was that I was applying unreasonable standards to myself in assuming I would be competent immediately.

The lesson, of course, was that I was not allowing myself to be a beginner, and that if I would do so, I would be less frustrated, I would learn more quickly and I would be a happier person. Now, each time I am a beginner in a new area, I recall the silk scarves on the floor. *As you begin this new and exciting process of building a family team, I ask you to do the same.*

1 Preparation

George Huntington Hartford II, heir to the A & P fortune, typifies the heir who was unprepared to receive wealth. Hunt, as he was known to his friends, was so isolated from the family business that he was in total ignorance of it when he inherited a ninety-million-dollar fortune. He hadn't been allowed to participate in financial affairs and had been given no instruction at all in money management. Wanting to make good use of his inheritance but not knowing how to go about it, Hunt indulged his one great interest—fine arts—by first investing in a California artists' colony which turned out to be a failure. His second major investment was an art magazine which soon folded. His third investment was an art museum in New York City which also failed. Even with many advisers around him, Hunt was bewildered. He couldn't distinguish the competent advisers from the incompetent ones, nor was he able to properly evaluate their advice. He spent thirty million dollars to develop an island resort in the Bahamas, but, shortsightedly, sold his interest before it became profitable. Hunt also spent huge sums on high living and drugs, which badly damaged his health.

Year after year, Hunt's fortune dwindled, the result of bad decisions, bad money management and imprudent habits. Today, only a fraction of the inheritance remains, and George Huntington Hartford II, living in isolation and poor health, looks back on a fortune for which he was unprepared and which proved to be his undoing.

The story of Hunt Hartford is not at all uncommon. Though you, yourself, have probably built up your own business and wealth, your sons and daughters will have to deal with money coming to them which they didn't earn. Affluence and the responsibilities that accompany wealth are part of their heritage. They didn't have a choice.

For all the sharp, tough, creative thought that business owners put into their businesses, they almost never approach the continuity of their business or their grown-up children's ability to oversee the family assets with the same determination. Is this the nature of things? Are your sons and daughters so different from you that they simply cannot acquire the skills you now have? Of course, each family is different, but based on my years of experience helping business owners put their affairs together, I can say with confidence that lack of preparation is the common denominator that causes so many problems, and that you *can* prepare your children to responsibly inherit your wealth as well as your values.

Preparing children takes time. Yet in the United States there is now a tremendous lack of long-term thinking. We read about it every-where—in business, where the quarterly report is the most important thing in the world; in politics, where the future extends only to the next election; and even in sports, where the current season's standing outweighs the need for long-term team improvement.

This tendency to look at just the short term is also present in our grown-up children. If you are 50-60 years old, and we assume a normal life expectancy of 75-80 years, why, they ask, do they need to start worrying about their inheritance now? Aren't you going to be around for another 20 years or so? Your sons and daughters have to be shown why it is important to prepare, and they need to understand that it takes time—preparation to inherit wealth isn't something that will happen overnight.

Even as we pursue our short-term interests, most of us still have a longing in the back of our minds for continuity, for a bridge to the future. I'm reminded of a charming story from Japan, about a man who walked along a rural road to and from his workplace. Each day, during his walk, he noticed a farmer treading on a water wheel in order to flood a rice paddy. But nothing was ever planted there. This went on year after year for twenty years until, when they were both old, the first man asked the farmer, "Why are you doing this?" And the farmer replied, "I'm preparing this field for my grandson."

Many Americans do not plan adequately for the future. When we do, it's usually limited to our own lifetime. But if you have built up wealth or a business that provides jobs for people, turns out quality products or services and provides good income for your family... wouldn't it be a shame for all of that to disintegrate when it could continue to thrive and be a benefit to the world and to your heirs for generations?

Of course, passing on your wealth is much more than giving your grown-up children the ability to mind the store. What values will be passed on to them? Will money be more important to them than mutual consideration and respect? If so, there is a good chance that your grown-up children will initiate lawsuits against each other, as happens frequently with inheritees. Do your grown-up children think that money is simply something to spend and have a good time with or do they understand that the possession of wealth confers upon them the responsibility to also use it for the good of others? Will your sons and daughters think of the family business simply as something that provides them with income, or will they be involved in its maintenance and further development? What fundamental values will you leave them as part of your legacy?

The greatest gifts you can leave your children are your personal values—your beliefs about honesty and consideration, straight-shooting, giving a dollar's work for a dollar earned, to name a few. Your own values have been tested throughout a lifetime of learning, making mistakes and picking yourself up to try again. These values have real worth, and many times in this book I'll be bringing up the subject of your values and how they affect your family.

Your personal values aren't the only ones we'll be looking at. By comparing your values with those of your spouse and your children, you'll discover shared family values. These family values can be used to form a family consensus and family priorities, which then lead to family actions. It's by performing family actions and working together as a team that your children will begin the long but fruitful path to becoming prepared to inherit wealth.

Like most parents, you've worked hard in the past and have created a successful business or other assets. But your children were not a part of that creation. Something is missing, and that something is the link which connects your past to your children's future. I like to call this necessary link "bridge building," where our values, our experiences and our creations become bridges which span the gaps between family members, between the family and the world, and between generations.

Before we continue with the next topic of communicating our values to our children, I'd like to share something with you which I hold in high esteem. Written in 1898, it's called:

The Bridge Builder

An old man, going a lone highway,
Came at the evening, cold and gray,
To a chasm, vast and deep and wide,
Through which was flowing a sullen tide.
The old man crossed in the twilight dim--
That sullen stream had no fears for him;
But he turned when he reached the other side,
And built a bridge to span the tide.
"Old man," said a fellow pilgrim near,
"You are wasting strength in building here.
Your journey will end with the ending day;
You never again must pass this way.
You have crossed the chasm, deep and wide,
Why build you the bridge at the eventide?"
The builder lifted his old gray head.
"Good friend, in the path I have come," he said,
"There followeth after me today
A youth whose feet must pass this way.
This chasm that has been naught to me
To that fair-haired youth may a pitfall be.
He, too, must cross in the twilight dim;
Good friend, I am building the bridge for him."

William Allen Dromgoole

2 Communication

I walked in and looked around before the meeting began. Seated in the room were Jim and Susan Weygand, Jim's son and daughter by a former marriage (both in their late 30's), and Susan's two sons, also by a former marriage (a little younger). The tentative subjects on the agenda were some portfolio decisions for the family investments.

This was not my first meeting with the Weygands, and we had all worked hard together to create a safe atmosphere for family communication. The ground rules I had established helped. These rules were: 1) Anyone can raise any point or ask any questions without repercussions, 2) Only problems can be attacked, not individuals, and 3) If anyone is uncomfortable introducing a subject, the facilitator will do it for him.

When the portfolio matters were concluded, Jim's daughter, Lucie, said, "There's something that Dad's been avoiding that really bugs us. Last year Dad told us he was going to change lawyers and get one that we could all work with, but he never did. I've asked him three times but nothing ever happens." Then Susan's older son, Wade, added, "Dad's lawyer has the same answer for everything we suggest—'I don't think that would be wise.' No matter what the subject is, it's always the same, 'I don't think that would be wise.' He treats us like schoolchildren. We just can't deal with that man."

Jim turned to me and grinned. We were both proud of the way his and Susan's grown-up children were beginning to assert themselves. But Jim wasn't going to give up easily, and he used a delaying tactic that had been successful in the past. He said: "You have a good point, but I don't think this is the proper time to discuss this." This authoritative declaration, coming from the "boss," had in the past been sufficient to stifle any further inquiry. This time it didn't work. These young adults knew the rules of this communication session, and stuck to them.

No sooner were the words out of Jim's mouth than Lucie said, "Wait a minute, Dad, you're breaking the rules—right Mr. Williams?" Then I turned to Jim and said, "She's right, Jim. This is an appropriate time to discuss it. She's raised a legitimate issue."

For a long time, Jim had kept his business cards close to his chest. The result was that no one else in the family knew what was happening. Here was an opportunity to break that pattern. Jim resisted at first, but then opened up. He explained about some difficult litigation that was in progress. The importance of the litigation, he felt, prevented him from changing lawyers. One of his sons responded with, "But we didn't know that," and Jim's wife, Susan, added: "I didn't know that either." The discussion became heated because there were a lot of repressed feelings being aired for the first time, but there was also a change from past family meetings. These family members were starting to communicate with each other—really communicate—for the first time since I'd met them.

From his side, Jim admitted he was used to making business decisions on his own, and that it just hadn't occurred to him to share this problem with his family. After discussing the litigation, Susan and all four sons and daughters agreed that it would have been wrong to change lawyers at that time. But they extracted a promise from their dad that he would tell them, from now on, if something happened to prevent him from keeping his word.

Jim wasn't used to being challenged—by anyone. When the meeting was over, Jim came up to me and said, "That's it, Roy, you've put me through the mill. I'm never going through this again." But just then the entire family approached Jim, and his daughter, Lucie, hugged him and said, "Dad, I guess I never knew until today that sometimes you really get bothered by problems too. I feel closer to you now than I have for a long time. Thanks for having this meeting."

I grinned at Jim and managed to keep quiet while we all savored the moment. A short while later, Jim and I scheduled the next meeting.

At a subsequent family meeting, the subject of the lawyer came up again. This time, there was a sound basis for making a family decision. Based on the needs of the business and some good input from all parties, the family decided to begin an immediate search for a new lawyer, with the stipulation that the present one would remain until the litigation was finished. This was a win-win situation. Everyone got something they wanted plus the whole family got something it needed—communication. It was a real turning point for the Weygands, because this was the first time they had ever pulled together for a common goal.

Over and over again I find that family members' perceptions of each other are inaccurate and hinder communication. One of my roles as facilitator is to make sure that family members are able to get their important messages into the open, clearly and honestly. I recall a meeting with Frank Russo and his 24-year-old son, Paul. Frank had divorced his wife several years earlier. During the meeting, Frank just blew up at his son. He shouted at him, "You go down to L.A. to see your mother, right? About once every few months, right? How many times have you called *me* in the last year? None! Not a single, damned time, and you live less than 20 miles away!"

Paul was taken aback, but he recovered quickly and shouted back in kind, "You're always too busy, so I stopped calling. Besides, I didn't think you cared!" There was a moment of quiet, and then I asked each of them to try to interpret what was really going on—what they had really meant under the harsh words.

As hurtful as this brief exchange was, Frank and Paul understood that beneath the accusations, father and son *did* care for each other; they just had to learn to express it in a better way. This exchange between them was a new beginning in being open and honest. Though much more communication between them was needed, it was a start toward acknowledging the real love they felt for each other.

Effective communication is an art. As Alfred Viera, a communications specialist of Business Design Associates puts it, "...the words that are spoken are never sufficient to provide all the meaning that a given speaker intends to convey."[1]

Some communication problems within families are due to different perceptions of roles. For example, in a business setting when a CEO father asks his accountant daughter to get him a cup of coffee, he is not just making a simple request. He is also sending a signal about the terms of the relationship and their history. He assumes that he has the right to ask her and that she will obey. But what if she were to reply, "No, Dad, why don't you ask one of the other vice-presidents?" or "That's a job for your secretary." Then they would be arguing over the rules of their relationship. She would be calling upon the assumptions of a work relationship, while he assumes the family relationship is still in effect."

In many families of affluence, where the father spends most of his time with the business, basic misperceptions often lead to conflicts. In family meetings, there is an exercise I use which demonstrates, with drawings of a young and an old woman, how differing perceptions can be reconciled.

First I show the drawing of the young woman to half the participants and the drawing of the old woman to the other half. Next I show a composite drawing to everyone. This composite combines elements of the young woman and the old woman into a single picture. Because of their previous impressions (from looking at the first drawing), the first half see a young woman in the composite, while the second half see the figure of the old woman. Then I show everyone the two original drawings and the composite, and we discuss them. After a few moments, all members of the group can see both faces in the composite. I use this simple principle to demonstrate that differing perceptions can be reconciled.

The Williams Group has developed several exercises for purposes of aiding communication. Exercises of this kind aren't just idle entertainment. They help build compromise and mutual understanding, and they are effective tools which show how perceptions can impact communication. When the family members have had some experience in reconciling simple, non-threatening perceptions like the exercise with the drawings, the next time there is a family conflict they are better prepared. For example, after going through a series of meetings, one family member threatened another by mentioning the possibility of a lawsuit. Before it got out of hand, the others said to him, "Yes, you have a point, but we don't need a lawsuit—let's see if we can reconcile this among ourselves."

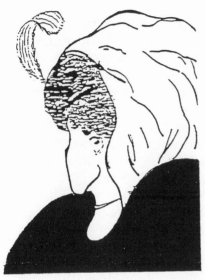

OLD WOMAN

YOUNG WOMAN

COMPOSITE

If basic trust exists between family members, then differing perceptions among family members are solvable problems. If I say a color is blue and you say it is green, there are several ways we can find a common ground. We can agree to call it blue-green, or we can agree to find a color chart and abide by its nomenclature. Whatever way we choose, there is an underlying assumption: that we both want a fair solution to our differences in perception. We trust each other enough to know that neither of us will try to cheat or harm the other in order to gain a decision in our favor. Similarly, in family disagreements, if there is basic trust between family members, differences in perception can usually be discussed and an agreement can be reached. Lack of trust, on the other hand, is a much more serious and difficult problem.

For example, if, for whatever reason, the children believe that their father or their mother have not keep their word on a particular matter, they'll probably believe that he or she can't be trusted in other matters as well. When family finances are discussed, that lack of trust can show up by their being argumentative and obstructionist. Family communication in general will be difficult and no one will know what the underlying problem is until the lack of trust is recognized and candidly discussed.

When a family comes together to resolve a conflict, it's important to find out as quickly as possible if the conflict is due to differing perceptions or to a lack of trust. If a lack of trust is the real basis for the disagreement, there can be no real communication until trust is reestablished. There are ways to build trust which I discuss in Chapter 6, but *re*building trust that has been lost requires a strong commitment by all family members.

Differing perceptions among family members are often prolonged because of taboo subjects. One of the aims of family communication is to eliminate as many subjects as possible from the list of unmentionables. Some of the subjects commonly taboo are: How much wealth does the family actually have? How will the family decide if the grown-up children are competent to handle wealth? How will the wealth be divided among the grown-up children? When is Dad going to retire and (if sons or daughters are going to become involved with the business) when will he give up control? What happens when Dad dies (or Mom, if she is the family entrepreneur)? What liabilities will the grown-up children incur when Mom and Dad are both dead? And how will the spouses of those children be treated without creating marital problems?

Other unmentionable areas are each family member's personal feelings about affection, hugging between father and son, anger, frustration, disappointment, distrust and the whole gamut of emotions which are generally repressed in family conversations. By allowing open discussion and the sharing of feelings there is a good chance that these emotions can be better understood.

During family meetings, it's interesting to observe that a subject is no longer taboo once there is a safe atmosphere for candid give-and-take and the subject has been openly discussed. Division of wealth and control among siblings is often unmentionable, initially. In one case, a family's younger daughter was more qualified than the older son to take over the family business. It took great effort to get the subject on the table, but once it was brought up, all kinds of questions could be asked. The son asked, "Can I live with my sister being president even though I'm older and I've been the big brother all of my life? Is there any position in the company that I can take with my sister as president? Should I just bail out of the business? If I bail, can I live with the fact that my sister will be making half a million bucks a year and I won't?"

These are the kinds of questions which must be asked. Sometimes, the answers won't be known for years. Ultimately, in the above case, the son might decide that he can't be in the same company while his sister is president. That's okay because it's honest. In that case, alternatives can be found which will allow the son to get out of the business but still receive some income from it that doesn't harm business operations. And if the son doesn't believe that his sister will run the company well enough to appreciate his share of the business assets over the long term, a buy-and-sell agreement can be arranged which is fair to all.

When Mom and Dad are older, and the grown-up children have become aware of the huge tax liability they will incur when both parents are gone, what can they do? Can they approach Mom and Dad and say, "We need to talk about your deaths"? They're afraid Mom and Dad will think: "You greedy kids, trying to get our money." And Mom and Dad don't want to talk about dying because it's uncomfortable. So everyone avoids the subject and, if nothing is done to plan otherwise, the kids receive such a large tax bill that the business may have to be sold or liquidated— sometimes at a fraction of its worth.

Sometimes, Mom and Dad are afraid to discuss certain topics. They may refuse to acknowledge, for example, that one of their sons acts foolishly and is not competent enough to take on business responsibilities. When this is the case, they are so habituated to treating all the children equally while they were growing up that it's very hard for them to do what is *right*. The parents are afraid of hurting their grown-up children's feelings, afraid of making them angry and afraid of being accused of unfairness. Unless they are able to discuss the situation and work out a reasonable solution, they are setting the stage for lawsuits between the siblings, and continuing bitterness.

Sometimes, a lack of communication results in unintended, or opposite, messages being sent. In one case, a client of mine, Tom Wilbanks, gave his daughter, Lynn, $10,000 to invest any way she desired. She immediately put the money into CD's and kept it there. For years, Tom had been griping about the stock market, about the incompetent managers of mutual funds, and about the questionable ethics in commodities trading. On top of that, Tom complained about the instability of real estate investments. Lynn got the clear (though unintended) message from all of this: "Investments are dangerous—play it safe." She was terribly afraid of making a mistake and losing *her Dad's money*, even though he had said it was hers. Aside from his skeptical comments about investments, her father had never tried to teach her anything about investing. He just assumed that she would somehow have this ability.

There was another Tom—Tom Tandy—who has a 19-year-old boy named Rick. Rick told me, "I don't trust my Dad." I asked him why, and he said, "Because he lied to me." "Come on," I said, "What did he lie about?" Rick said, "He told me that when I turned sixteen he would buy me a new car if I passed the driver's test. After I passed the test, I reminded him about the car and he said we couldn't afford it now—I'd have to wait. That company of his is worth more than ten million dollars and he can't afford a car? I'll never trust him again!"

Rick was nineteen when I met him. By a combination of earning money from a part-time job and help from his father, Rick had gotten his car a year later, but, secretly, he never forgave his father for going back on his word. The incident of a father having a cash crunch is not uncommon—it happens in all businesses from time to time. But in this case, Tom never took the time to explain that to his son—he was always too busy with business problems. Rick, for his part, never communicated his resentment to his father, and, after three years, his distrust has solidified. Today, Tom senses that his son holds a grudge against him but he is still too busy to find out why.

Learning to listen with the "third ear" is one of the requirements for good communication. But how does someone go about listening with the third ear? We have found that careful listening to the moods, concerns and other expressions in a person's voice helps to identify what is really going on. From this, we can begin to identify some of the underlying issues that are creating the problems.

If moods reflect our assessment of the future, then by listening for moods we may be better able to anticipate the actions someone may take (or lack of actions if the mood is one of resignation or despair). By sensitive listening, we can help learn and plan the actions which will be needed to resolve those concerns.

In their book on family relationships, Drs. Jordan and Margaret Paul state it like this: "All of the many varieties of responses to a conflict come from only two basic motives or intentions: 1) the intent to learn—an openness to learning from the conflict, which leads to loving behavior, or 2) the intent to protect—defending against any potential pain that might come from the conflict, which leads to unloving behavior. Any response other than an openness to learning is a protection."[1]

In all of our family meetings, when there is a conflict, I make sure that I say, "Look, I don't know if what you're saying is real. Is this how you really feel, or do you want to say something else? Are you possibly speaking from some kind of fear...fear of offending someone, fear of looking foolish, or fear of facing something unpleasant?" All of these mask the person's true feelings and prevent effective communication.

Getting all of the family members informed is one of the goals of these discussions. Yet some business owners deliberately try to keep other family members uninformed. Last year, a woman asked me to look into her finances. Her husband had recently died without having told her anything about the state of their affairs, and she literally didn't know if she had enough money to buy food. He had been a scheming old codger who had liquidated most of his assets except his business. He had a son who was involved in the business, but before the father had died, he had sold the business out from under his son without telling him. The mother had no idea any of this was happening. When we investigated her assets, it turned out she was quite wealthy. Communication had been her husband's lowest priority, even as he faced death.

Sometimes both parents conspire to keep their children uninformed. It's like this with Phil and Jessie Kronner who live in Southern California. Their net worth is something like 30 million dollars. They don't discuss money with their children. When I asked them why, they said, "Because the kids (aged 20 and 23) aren't ready." Phil and Jessie are even reluctant to talk about money with each other. The problem is, they don't like to think of themselves as being rich—it embarrasses them. Whatever the reason, their children are grown up now but they are still uninformed. Not only are the son and daughter ignorant about handling wealth, the subliminal message they receive from their parents is, "We don't trust you."

In family after family, I find what most children want is more communication—especially with a reticent Dad. When the children get to pick Dad's brain and find out what's really happening with the business and investments, it becomes very exciting. When all family members are informed, the whole family gets excited, especially when advisers are brought into the family meetings. We bring the banker, the lawyer and the accountant to the meeting, and we listen to them. Everyone hears how Dad deals with them. Sometimes Dad or Mom won't accept the advice of an adviser—for rational or irrational reasons. For example, Dad may say that he doesn't want to sign a will, but he is unwilling to give his reasons. After much prodding, his true feelings begin to surface and he admits that he has a feeling that if he signs a will, he will die, because his sister died one day after she signed her will. That's okay because it is honest communication, from the heart. In this case, we were able to get Dad to create a living trust so he didn't have to sign a will. But the important thing is that Dad has been open and honest, so everyone in the family knows what is going on.

I recall an especially good communications breakthrough in Bill Coleman's family. Bill and his wife are socially responsible people, and they've accomplished much good with their money. They have two sons and three daughters. The social responsibility has rubbed off on the daughters but not—at least not yet—onto the sons. At one of our first meetings, the daughters wanted the family to stop investing in South African companies (this was before the recent changes in South African social policies), but the sons ridiculed them.

"Who cares about apartheid? Let those guys down there shoot each other." It was the same thing when the daughters wanted to cancel a family investment in a Northwest lumber company as a protest against cutting down old-growth forests. The sons countered with, "Those people up there are nearly starving to death...they need the jobs more than they need to save the trees. Besides, you don't have all the facts." The sons kept ridiculing the daughters in a heavy-handed way and the meeting got very emotional. The daughters cried, and complained that the sons always got their way, that Mom and Dad never listened to them. There were too many strong passions flying around to accomplish anything at that moment, and there was too little factual information. The daughters, though sincere, were not presenting their case in a way that the other family members could respect. I suggested that they compile an information file and document their causes, including the consequences of removing selected investments from the family portfolio.

So the daughters started gathering social and environmental data to back up their positions, and, with help from Dad, the effects divesting would have on their portfolio. At the next family meeting, the daughters presented their information to their brothers and to both parents. Their presentation was well received by all family members. The fact that the daughters were now presenting their views in a more reasoned manner helped to soften the social perceptions of the sons considerably, and brought them closer to the daughters. Eventually, a compromise was reached. The daughters chose the five most important investments to eliminate from the family's portfolio, and everyone accepted that. This was the beginning of a more trusting relationship between all family members. It didn't happen overnight—it took about one year before they all began to really trust each other's opinions, but the end results were very satisfying, and everyone grew from the experience.

In their book, *If You Really Loved Me,*[2] Jordan and Margaret Paul speak out on communication: "Loving behavior cannot occur merely by a decision to be more loving. Why? Because standing in the way for every person are some very powerful, deeply ingrained fears and false beliefs which block the love everyone is capable of giving. Overcoming these beliefs requires your dedication to a process of confronting these beliefs and changing them."

Communication is one of the necessary first steps that lead to the effective transfer of wealth and wisdom. I start the family communication process by holding formal family meetings (which are described in more detail in the next chapter). With good communication helping to create mutual trust, a family will be more and more able to talk about taboo subjects which need to be brought out onto the table. When sensitive topics are discussed, repressed fear and anger felt by family members are often revealed and can be addressed. In fact, learning to listen and to hear what each person is really saying goes a long way toward having effective communication.

The result of this more effective communication is an increasingly informed family, a family that is starting to pull together and to develop mutual trust. This is one of the most rewarding things that can happen to your family, and its benefits will reach into every aspect of your lives.

1, 2   Paul, Jordan and Margaret, *If You Really Loved Me,* Compcare Publishers, Minneapolis, MN, 1987

3 The Family Advisory Board

James Keel's family is about to convene a meeting of its Family Advisory Board. Sarah Keel, James' wife, has agreed to chair the meeting, her first as Chairman. The Keels' three grown-up children—two daughters and a son are there (ages, 27, 25 and 24). Also present at this meeting are their lawyer and their accountant. And finally, a family facilitator, a person skilled in guiding these meetings, is attending.

Mom calls the meeting to order and distributes agendas to those who have not already seen them. The first topic is how to proceed with forming a family partnership. Dad begins by explaining the purpose of the partnership and then asks the lawyer a series of questions. The lawyer answers the first question but then he tries to cover his lack of preparation by waffling. Dad is right on top of him and won't let the lawyer get away with this. Mom, the daughters and the son listen closely; this is a side of their dad they've never seen—how he deals with his advisers. The lawyer then promises to get the desired information to the family within the week, and Dad thanks him courteously for his input.

Mom then brings up the next topic on the agenda, which is to discuss who among the three grown-up children are now willing to definitely commit themselves to joining the family business. Dad starts to dominate the conversation but the facilitator interrupts and says, "Wait a minute, Jim, everyone needs a chance to speak for themselves. Let's let them do it, one at a time." There is a moment of silence. Dad is the boss of a very large company, and his daughters and son have never heard anyone speak to him like this. But Dad complies and says, "Okay," and the daughters and the son, in turn, hesitantly give their views on joining the business.

Katie, the oldest daughter, addresses Dad: "I don't know if I want to be involved. You've always been so secretive about the business that I have no idea what it's really like." The others add similar charges aimed at Dad. He cringes but grins. In spite of the criticism, he is pleased that his son and daughters are able to stand up to him. Dad says, "Alright, we can fix that. On Thursday morning, 9:00 a.m. sharp, we're all going on a grand tour of the plant." Will, the youngest of the siblings, has become emboldened. He says, "Dad, I'd like to see the sales and profit figures as well as the physical plant." Dad cringes again, then replies, "Can we do the tour first? I'd like to handle one thing at a time." His children agree, feeling they have pushed their dad enough at this time, but making mental notes to bring this up at the next family board meeting. Mom then gives a summary of what has been accomplished and what each participant is expected to do, within a given time frame, as a result of the meeting. Mom then adjourns the meeting of the Family Advisory Board.

Of course, this brief description tells only a small portion of everything that happened at this eight hour meeting, but it illustrates the nature of the proceedings and the kinds of things that can be accomplished with a Family Advisory Board. For example, the family members were introduced to three of Dad's closest advisers: his lawyer, his accountant and his family facilitator. They've seen how he operates with them. Mom learned more about the family business and, through her chairing the meeting, has gained a sense of sharing control of important family matters. Perhaps most important of all, the son and daughters found a safe forum for speaking candidly to their parents about things that disturbed them or which they wanted to know more about. And for the first time in years, the members of the Keel family began to really communicate with each other.

The Family Advisory Board is the best way my staff and I have found to create an atmosphere for real communication within the family. These meetings are not for casual, daily decisions of the family, but for addressing important topics and dealing with the strong feelings they produce. The Family Advisory Board isn't a legally-constituted board of directors, it's just a way of formalizing family meetings which offers several advantages. First, the formality of the meeting says to sons and daughters that this isn't just another discussion Mom and Dad have called together to decide what color to paint their kitchen. Second, having an agenda encourages the participants to think seriously about the topics. Third, the presence of persons from outside the family augments the seriousness of the meeting's purpose.

While the agenda gets everyone thinking, the course of the meeting need not follow it inflexibly. For example, a family may meet to talk about a family partnership but as the discussion warms up, the subject of real interest turns out to be a divorce that happened five years ago, and the anger that the sons and daughters still feel about it.

The Family Advisory Board consists of all family members, including young children who are mature enough not to disrupt the proceedings. It can either include or exclude spouses of grown-up children; the family members have to decide whether or not in-laws should participate. *The family facilitator attends all board meetings.* This is because the family will be dealing with difficult topics and may not be able to handle them constructively by themselves. The facilitator may also introduce new ways of looking at problems and provide options not considered before. Also attending, on an as-needed basis, are the key executives of the family business: the lawyer, accountant, money manager, and so on. Each one of these managers or specialists addresses the group regarding his area of expertise. Even family members who are hostile attend. Though they may disagree with what's going on, they still want to know what's happening and to be where the action is. Of all my clients through the years, I've never had a single family member refuse to attend family board meetings, once they found out what what was happening.

Hostile family members, or amiable family members who have suppressed their feelings, find a safe forum in the Family Advisory Board. In these meetings, it's acceptable to show anger, fear and frustration. It's also okay to express love, compassion and understanding, which are often absent in daily family life. The board meetings are a safe haven for disagreeing with Mom and

Dad. This is where it is alright for younger and grown-up children to express personal values and beliefs, and to test Mom's and Dad's beliefs, because they are testing them not as their children but as members of the board.

This is a forum where touchy subjects can be discussed. For example if a son and his wife need more money and want to sell some of their stock, they have to understand that it is going to decrease their capital, which means a decrease in earning power. Everyone needs to understand that, over the long term, a considerable amount of potential income will be lost by selling shares now. The only way grown-up children and their spouses are going to learn this is by candidly discussing it.

In addition to the currently-participating members of the Family Advisory Board, I recommend that the entrepreneur of the family select individuals who will act as advisers to the family if he or she dies. I first got this idea many years ago, working with Peggy Fletcher. Peggy's husband, Brad, had been ill for three years before he died. During those last three years he had neglected the business and, at the time of his death, the company was in deep trouble with three million dollars of debt obligations. The debt was burying it.

Peggy called me one day and said, "Roy, I'm in trouble. My lawyer and my accountant say I have to file for bankruptcy. I need your help." On the next Saturday morning, when I arrived at her home, several other businessmen, whom I knew, were also there. We had all been asked to help. We worked all day on finding ways to get around bankruptcy. When we were finished, Peggy had a plan to save the company.

Later, I wondered if *my* wife would have had the presence to call, and if so, who would she have called, and would they be the same ones I would recommend? From that day forward, I have instituted this arrangement in my own family and those of our clients.

In general, we recommend that five advisers be chosen (the number chosen can be other than five, but I've found that this generally works best; you want an odd number to avoid tie votes, seven starts to get unwieldy, and three persons may be too few to do the job effectively.)

How do you choose the advisers to help your family in case of your death? While it is helpful for these advisers to have some familiarity with business, finance, banking and investments, the most important thing is that they are persons who have gained your family's trust. You need to be able to trust in their integrity, their common sense and, when they don't know something, their ability to find the right answers. At least once a year, all of these five advisers should attend a family board meeting so your spouse and children can get to know them and feel comfortable with them as well.

When a Family Advisory Board is created, it usually meets once a quarter for the first few years. After that, the frequency may slow to about twice a year, depending on the needs of the particular family. Once each year, there is a special annual board meeting. The entire family and all advisers should attend this annual meeting, as well as key executives of the business. Each executive delivers a state-of-the-business report for his area of responsibility, and the business owner gives a summary of it all. In this way, the professional advisers know what's going on and can do their jobs better, and the spouse and children get to see the often-mysterious world of the family business.

When a family sits down together at a board meeting, no subject is off limits. The daughter may bitterly resent Dad and Mom's willingness to pay for her MBA but their refusal to give her a penny for acting school. Or Mom may see Dad's health declining and be terribly worried because he won't let up on his business schedule. When these kinds of subjects come up, the fur begins to fly. And because Dad is usually the strong, assertive, entrepreneurial type, he dominates the discussions and the other family members are intimidated.

Here is where an objective intermediary—the family facilitator—can be of real help. A facilitator is someone who not only has the experience to help the family plan for the transfer of their wealth, but who also has the skills and sensitivity to guide the family communication process in a productive direction. One advantage the facilitator has is that he can't be bullied—he has the credentials, the authority and the toughness, when required, to let a family member know when he or she is out of line. Another advantage is objectivity. Often, family members are so involved that they lose sight of what they are trying to accomplish. A brief reminder from the facilitator keeps things on track.

A skilled facilitator can hear things that slip by family members. Frequently, Mom or Dad will give opinions out of long habit, without really believing what they are saying. When the facilitator questions them closely on this, it often turns out they are avoiding a difficult issue. Dad may be having problems with the business which are taking a lot of his time and energy, or he may be having difficulties with his wife, children or grandchildren. When this is the case, it's hard to get him to focus on a family issue that he's managed to sweep under the rug for years. Also, it can be a very painful process. In one family, the father made a judgment call which skirted the edge of good ethics. His sons called him on it and wanted a thorough airing of the matter. Dad resisted strongly until the facilitator finally said to him, privately, "This is creating a problem. If you don't face it, this issue will haunt you for the rest of your life and your sons will distrust you from now on." As is most often the case, once the issue was brought out on the table, it wasn't nearly as serious as either the sons or Dad had imagined it, and the whole problem was resolved.

Sometimes, as facilitator, I speak privately to each family member about a particular subject before it is brought up in a family board meeting. This prepares them for it, and defensive reactions have a chance to cool down. Because the facilitator is the one who, however tactfully, introduces a subject and forces the family to address it, he is often the scapegoat. I've borne the wrath of strong-willed dads many times, but it's worth being the "bad guy" when the benefits are so impressive. Invariably, when family members work through a painful but necessary discussion with the aid of a facilitator, they become closer when it is finished.

Usually, it is the children who have a hard time bringing up delicate subjects with their parents, but sometimes it is the other way around. A recent example is Stanley and Wilma Erlich. The Erlich's estate is worth about 40 million dollars, and they want to pass it on through their bloodline. That is, they don't want sons-in-law or daughters-in-law to be inheritors. What they want to avoid is having money leave their bloodline if there is a divorce some time in the future. They were afraid to bring up this issue because they didn't want to hurt anyone's feelings or disrupt their grown-up children's marriages. I was able to help, as facilitator, because I was a neutral party and could raise the issue without being accused of favoritism.

In another meeting with the Erlich family, we discussed distributing their wealth among four grown-up children, all of whom are married. There was potential for conflict here. One of the sons had done several things to embarrass the family, and he was known to be flighty and unrealistic. Stanley was very apprehensive about letting him have any control over substantial parts of their assets. I began by handing out copies of a list of definitions of competence levels. This list described various levels of competence from beginning to highly-skilled levels.

Then we listed, on an easel pad, the areas where family members were concerned about competence. These areas included such things as money management, property management, requirements for company president, succession planning and parent-child relations. For each of these areas of concern, I asked all family members to evaluate their skill levels. In a situation like this, no one addresses the less capable, less respected individual and says, "You are incompetent." On the contrary, each family member reads the descriptions for the different levels of competence and chooses the level which most closely corresponds to their skills. Because there is no external criticism or other pressure being placed on them, the participants tend to evaluate themselves honestly and fairly.

In this way, the less competent individual can be candid about himself while still maintaining the "cover" of an abstract discussion. In the process, the other members of the family learn how he wants to be treated. The less competent individual will usually acknowledge that his role in the control of family wealth should not necessarily be the same as the other siblings, *as long as he has some kind of role.*

Because all of this has been brought out into the open, the family's perceptions begin to change. The black sheep is no longer quite so black and is no longer automatically labeled as incompetent. Now he seems more like someone who is special and who can make some kind of acceptable contribution to the family. This allows the less capable individual some dignity and helps to build his confidence. In spite of his limitations, he is starting to be perceived as part of the team instead of as an obstacle. It is a win-win situation.

Sometimes the entrepreneur of the family is so close to a situation he can't see that he is caught in a pattern of repeating errors. Then the job of the facilitator is to point this out to him. This happened with David Meltzer, who owns a very large company on the West Coast. Dave, together with his brother and sister, inherited equal shares of a business that was worth hundreds of millions of dollars. Dave ran the business; his brother and sister weren't involved. When Dave turned 60, the brother and sister wanted to cash out and they forced him to sell the company. Dave was angry and felt betrayed after the many years he'd spent building it up. After the sale, Dave picked himself up again and started a new company with his oldest son. When I met Dave, the company was doing five million dollars in annual sales, after only two years, so it had grown rapidly.

In addition to his son, who helps run the company, Dave has a younger son and a daughter. When I asked him how he was going to share his wealth with his children, he said, "I'm going to give one-third to each of the kids." I laughed and said, "Dave, do you realize what you're setting up? You just told me five minutes ago how angry you were with your brother and sister, and now you're telling me you're going to do the same thing with your kids?" Dave was dumfounded. Until that moment, this sharp, highly talented businessman was totally unaware that he had set the stage for a repetition of the same kind of sibling bitterness he, himself, had experienced.

The skilled facilitator can often make a dramatic difference in the lives of his clients. A story about a business owner of long ago illustrates this nicely. This particular businessman was in transportation—specifically, camels. He had reached a point in his life where he was ready to turn his business over to his three sons. His assets were seventeen camels.

His oldest son was diligent and dutiful, so the businessman set aside half his camels for him. His second son, though not so diligent, was creative and thoughtful. He got one-third of the camels. The youngest son never took anything seriously and was likely to squander his inheritance, so the father set aside only a ninth portion for him.

The businessman had a succession plan drawn up for him by his legal advisers and then picked an auspicious day for the transfer of his wealth. When the day approached, he thought about his seventeen camels and suddenly realized he had made a terrible mistake. With seventeen camels, it was impossible to divide them in half, third and ninth portions. But his legal advisers told him the succession plan was binding and must go through.

Having heard of a wise man, he went to see him and explained his problem. The wise man told him not to worry—that he would take care of the problem on the day of the succession. When that day arrived, the three sons were busy counting the camels they were to receive, scratching their heads and arguing noisily. Their father waited anxiously until the wise man arrived. Curiously, the wise man, himself, was leading a camel.

"Greetings," said the wise man, "I have brought you my camel. I will give him to you for the next few minutes and that will solve your problem." The father, now more anxious than ever, groaned and asked, "How can that possibly solve my problem?" "Notice," said the wise man, that you now own eighteen camels. Half of them is nine. Give nine camels to your oldest son. One-third of your camels is six. Give six camels to your middle son. A ninth portion of your camels is two. Give two camels to your youngest son. You have now fulfilled your pledge to your sons, and you have given away seventeen of your eighteen camels. Now give me back the eighteenth camel and the job is done."

This facilitator had made a difference.

While Dad is the information source regarding the business, and the facilitator offers insight and guidance, Mom also has an important role to play on the Family Advisory Board. I usually recommend that Mom chair the family board. When I first suggest this, many moms try to get out of it. For one thing, the formal procedure of the meetings may make her uncomfortable because she is unused to adhering to procedural rules. But there is a reason for these formalities. By doing things formally, the procedures are consistent. If someone disagrees with what is happening during a meeting, or with anyone's right to introduce a subject, parliamentary rules generally prevail. These rules are good levelers of the playing field. They allow both younger and grown-up children to participate on a more equal footing with their parents and they help to insulate the children from Dad's domination of the meeting.

Mom may also be uncomfortable as Chairman because she is unused to dealing with professional authority figures. It is a new experience for her to call everyone to order, including lawyers, executives and other advisers that may be present. Also, some wives (or husbands) are so habituated to allowing their spouses to take the lead in public, especially in matters pertaining to business, that it is hard for them to take control of the meeting in the presence of their husband.

But in fact, Mom is probably better qualified than anyone else in the family to chair the family board meetings. She has been managing conflicts within the family for years, even though she hasn't done it formally. She is so used to instinctively dealing with the family that she doesn't realize how effective she is. After a while, Mom will start to realize that even though the meeting proceedings are formal, she is basically doing the same thing she already does every day with her husband and children. As she becomes more accustomed to her role, Mom brings into play all of her subtle social skills: sensing when to press for something and when to back off; knowing how to give encouragement when it is needed; detecting when someone is disingenuous; and being able to make use of the strengths and weaknesses of each member of the family.

With Mom as Chairman of the Family Advisory Board, Dad is still a powerful participant, of course. *But he is a participant, not the sole decision-maker.* To a large degree, Dad, by virtue of his business experience, is still the one who provides most of the information, but he has no control over the formal workings of the board.

Mom's chairing of the family board is by no means an idle pursuit. She is getting practice at what she may have to do in the future. If Dad should suddenly die, she will be more competent and more comfortable in dealing with professional advisers and business executives. Also, in this role, Mom is learning how to bring in consultants when additional information is needed in order to make decisions.

Children also make real contributions to family board meetings. When your children are still young—nine or ten years old—or later on, when your grandchildren are around that age, try taking them with you to business meetings. Even if they just sit there like little mice, the complexion of the meeting is changed. The adults not only use cleaner, more careful language, they go to great lengths to explain things clearly. The whole atmosphere of the meeting is lighter and more pleasant.

Taking both young and older children to meetings, including those of the Family Advisory Board, is a great education for them. It is an investment in their future. Not only that, when they feel comfortable they'll begin asking some interesting questions. Sometimes they'll ask questions that *you* are uncomfortable asking but which should be asked. I attended one meeting with a father, his 18-year-old daughter and his money manager. During the meeting, the money manager used the expression, "capitalization rate." The father was an experienced businessman but he wasn't familiar with that expression (he told me after the meeting). Not wanting to display his naivete, he decided to let it pass, but his daughter asked the money manager, "What does 'capitalization rate' mean?" Not only did the money manager have to explain the term, he had to explain it clearly and simply enough so that this young woman could understand it. In the process, her father also learned something.

Children are also good at picking up the feelings, moods and attitudes of adults in a group. Sometimes when an adviser reports to a family, one of the children may later say that they don't trust that person. This can be a great time for the family to learn more about trust, and to discuss the basis for trusting or not trusting. Many times, a child will detect insincerity. If the family agrees with this perception, it may be appropriate to replace the adviser or at least make him or her aware of the breakdown in trust, and provide an opportunity to improve it. The most important issue here is not only for children to listen to opinions, but to judge their credence. This will enhance the children's self-esteem and help them to learn about trust.

A way of sharpening grown-up children's skills is to have a rotating chairman of the family board, so that each sibling gets a chance, not just trying it once as a novelty, but long enough to develop skill at controlling the meeting. When you see this in action, it is immediately apparent what a dynamite idea it is and what confidence it gives these young adults.

Sometimes, when Dad dominates the meeting in spite of Mom's position as Chairman, the grown-up children are able to work together to push through a decision that is right. This happened to Jim Weygand's family, where there were three sons and one daughter. Toward the end of the meeting, Jim suddenly announced that he had chosen his oldest son, Evan, to become president of the company. The company was an automobile parts distributorship, with forty outlets and twenty million dollars in annual sales. After Jim's announcement, the whole room became silent. It was a surprise to everyone, including Mom and two of Jim's closest advisers. Evan, the subject of the announcement, didn't look pleased either. After a moment, Evan said, very tentatively, "Look, Pop, Lucie is really the most capable executive. I think she should be president." Jim got angry at that and shouted, "No way. I'm not going to have a girl president. Besides, Lucie doesn't want to be president." After that, things got pretty heated, and Mom was hard pressed to keep the meeting in order. But because of the procedural rules, everyone was able to speak their mind. When the daughter, Lucie, got a chance to talk, she was calm but very firm: "Pop, you never asked me. You asked all of the boys if they were interested but you never once mentioned the possibility to me. Well now you know. I *do* want to be president."

Jim didn't cave in all at once on this issue. Lucie's desire to be president was as much a shock to him as his announcement had been to the family. To his credit, he retreated graciously by saying he'd have to think about it until the next family board meeting, three months later. During that time, everyone worked on him. His wife, Susan, worked on him. All four siblings worked on him, and even I worked on him. At the next board meeting, Jim agreed that Lucie was the best choice for president, and everyone was pleased. It was another win-win situation. This particular event is an example of how grown-up children can become empowered. Not only does their collective wisdom often result in good decisions, they also learn the value of mutual support, of standing together for a good cause.

Hostile family members, surprisingly, usually make very good board members. The one who is the perennial irritant, who asks antagonistic questions and seems to be deliberately obstructive, is actually making an important contribution. First, his presence teaches the family how to deal with the anger and frustration that are disruptive to the proceedings. Second, and more importantly, what this angry person is saying may really be significant. He isn't afraid to challenge the system or to point up personal errors. If the other family members can learn to wade through the anger, they'll often find that there is some truth in the criticism. Mom, who is chairing the meeting, should encourage everyone to listen to what's being said and to try to ignore the anger. Gradually, as the angry person's views are heard and evaluated fairly, he'll begin to feel that it isn't necessary to be disruptive in order to be heard and respected. When this happens, the rest of the group will discover that individual is starting to become a more productive member.

This is a powerful lesson in communication—a real growth experience for the family.

After the family board meeting has ended, and all non-family members have left, I ask the entire family to have a debriefing session. I strongly encourage them to do this without me there. In this way, they can freely discuss my input and my role in the meeting, and my observations. I want the family to talk about what happened at the meeting—what was actually said and what was meant between the lines. Dad, as the business expert, or

Mom, as the case may be, will explain business issues to the rest of the family. Because there may have been other issues involved, including personal matters, it is important that each family member be able to share his or her observations. I also ask the family to discuss each participant's contribution to the meeting. If the business is involved, I ask the family to find out what specific actions Dad or Mom will take as a result of the meeting.

This debriefing session benefits everyone. The family begins to understand that advisers advise and that executives are the ones who execute, or implement, decisions. In evaluating the role of facilitator, and the give-and-take between him and the advisers, the family will start to see the specialized focus of these professionals and why, by definition, their roles are limited. Mom, as Chairman, ends the debriefing session by making up an action list—the steps the family will take as a result of the meeting. If further information is needed to undertake an action, that's okay, if acquiring the necessary information becomes one of the action steps. The point is, the family shouldn't drift back to the status quo as a result of the board meeting, but should spell out specific actions to be taken, who is responsible for implementing them, and on what timetable.

The Family Advisory Board is a very, very powerful tool. It creates a safe harbor in which to communicate. Within this safe atmosphere, the input of a skilled facilitator; the skills learned by Mom as Chairman; the experience and knowledge input from Dad; the learning to deal with advisers; and the education of young to grown-up children by actively participating—all these will give a strong boost to bringing the family closer together, in defining goals and in seeing those goals accomplished.

4 Introducing Your Business to Your Family

Almost twenty years ago, I was having lunch with a friend, who asked me: "Why are you in the business you are in today?" At first it seemed to be a simple question that deserved an equally simple answer. But as I began to think about it, I decided I needed a bit more time. So I replied, "I'll call you by 4:00 this afternoon and give you my answer." I wrote a couple of paragraphs that afternoon but I really wasn't happy with them. The more I thought about why I was in business, the more the question bothered me. When 4:00 p.m. came, I called my friend and said, "I don't have a good answer yet, but when I do, I'll call you." I'm sure I heard a soft chuckle as he hung up.

First, my family came to mind, and I thought: "It's for my family—I'm in business to build a future for my family." But as soon as I thought it over, I knew that that was not the real reason. As I asked myself the question over and over, other questions came to mind: Am I in business to build retirement? Is it for the challenge of the chase? Is it because I can't stand not acting on my ideas, and for that reason I won't work for anyone else?

Weeks went by, then a month. I would wake up at two or three in the morning with a new idea that was only part of the answer.

The trouble was, all of my answers were a part of the reason for my being in business, but not the *essential* reason. It took me months of reflecting to finally understand why I was really in business. Six months after he had asked me, I telephoned my friend with an answer.

I finally realized that the thing that really put passion into my work, what really provided fulfillment, was being able to significantly improve the lives of my clients and their families. That is the *essential reason* why I am in business.

Now I am passing the question on to you. Why are you in business today? Is it for your family? Is it because you enjoy the day-to-day operations? Is it the challenge of competition? What is the purpose of all the energy and creativity which you give to your business? Your business is something to which you're giving the lion's share of the hours of each week, almost every week of your life. Why?

It's not only important to know the answer for yourself, but for your children to know it as well. Often, children, when they are growing up, get a mistaken impression of the business because they hear only the negative details that dad or mom voice to let off steam. Many children, especially the children of wealthy parents, are asking: "What does our family business contribute to the world that is worthwhile?" They don't understand all of the positive aspects of the business that you take for granted because you are so involved with it. Often, even when they are grown-up, children don't realize the impact of the business on the lives of your employees, on the businesses of your suppliers and on the welfare of your customers.

How can you expect young adults to get fired up about being a part of the business if they don't really have an understanding of its purpose? How can they make intelligent decisions about whether or not to get involved until they know something about it?

A good place to start is to tell your children about how and why you first started the business. As facilitator at family board meetings, I'll ask questions about how the business got started. I'll ask questions such as: What was the original reason for starting the business? How did Dad select the industry? Was he apprehensive? What critical changes did Dad have to make in the business? What were the turning points? How has the position of the business in the marketplace evolved? Did Dad know how to set goals and accomplish them or was there some measure of trial and error?

I also ask Dad what important values he has instilled in the business. Are these values really upheld throughout the company, and do the executives believe in them? If not, could it be because Dad, himself, is not living the values he espouses? This point about values is very important because the children, young or grown-up, will be strongly influenced by whether or not Dad actually lives his values and, consequently, whether or not he really believes them.

I'll ask Dad about his own shortcomings. When did he guess wrong? What were some of his major mistakes? Sam Nomura comes to mind, and the one substantial mistake he made which nearly ruined him. I was at a family meeting with Sam, his wife, Connie, and their two boys, and I said, "Sam, tell the boys about the time when your dad let you buy some property, and what happened after that." Sam groaned and said, "Ouch! It still hurts to remember that. It was over twenty years ago, and I came real close to going belly-up."

"I wanted to buy 700 acres and my Dad put up the down payment and arranged the financing. I wanted to build a real nice subdivision. You know, wide streets, recreation center, three and four bedroom houses with large family rooms. Good quality construction. They were gonna go for $100,000—this was 1965. Well, I had sold a few houses but just as the work was almost completed, interest rates went through the roof and there was a housing slump...not just here, but all over the country.

"On top of that, I was overextended, trying to do too much with the money I had available. Well, I was scared, real scared. I didn't think I could meet payroll, and my suppliers...I felt awful about making them wait, but I just couldn't pay them. I went to the banks and tried to get additional financing. They kept telling me, 'You can't do it. You're not going to make it.' I was very angry at these guys, and I remember telling them, 'I *am* going to make it!' But all I got back was, 'Not with our money you're not.' "

By this point in the family meeting, Sam's sons were all ears. Even his wife, Connie, hadn't realized how difficult that period had been for her husband. They all wanted to know how he got out of it, and Sam continued: "I worked my rear off, even poured concrete myself. I sold off some lots to get cash for payroll. And I won't say I lied outright to the banks, but I sure stretched the truth. I finally got a bit more money out of them, and things started to turn around. I sold a few more houses and finally managed to pay off the suppliers. Then the market picked up again. But for a while, it was real close."

Sam said his mistake was in overextending himself and in neglecting to set up additional credit lines for contingencies. That was a relatively small mistake. I recall a bigger one—a giant size mistake. I'm thinking of Hugh Porter, who was in the oil drilling business. Hugh lost 31 million dollars. He was in the process of turning over his business to his grown-up children when there was an opportunity for a deal, and Hugh went for it. We were at a family board meeting when Hugh told his wife and children: "I just lost 31 million bucks of your money. It wasn't the lawyer's fault and it wasn't the accountant's fault. It was all me. My instinct told me there was something wrong but I ignored it. Kids, I really screwed up."

As large an amount as it was, the significant thing about this mistake is that it brought the family closer together. As in Sam Nomura's case, until Hugh's children learned about some of the business errors their father had made, they thought their dads walked on water, and that they could do no wrong. These meetings where Dad opens up and tells about his errors are real eye-openers. What extraordinarily powerful lessons! Dad says, "I screwed up. I accept the responsibility. It wasn't anyone else's fault—it was my fault." That's teaching the children accountability. It's teaching that it's okay to make mistakes and that, instead of blaming someone else for your mistakes, you admit them forthrightly and then you pick yourself up and try again. With Hugh Porter's business, Hugh and the children are working together to make up that 31 million dollar loss. Over the next few years, they'll probably make two or three times that amount. In the long run, that episode will turn out to be a plus for the family.

The image many sons and daughters have of their fathers is invincibility. Dad's perfect—they can never measure up to or equal Dad because they're human and he isn't. So when you acknowledge your mistakes and you admit to some of the human emotions of feeling guilty, depressed or culpable about having made them, your children see that you are human and vulnerable. This starts to build a climate of safety and trust within the family in which your children can be free to say anything. By seeing your vulnerability, you are letting your children know that it's okay if they make mistakes—nobody's perfect. And by showing that you, too, have real feelings, that you have problems you are concerned about, you're letting them know that you are human, just as they are.

Parents feel that they need to be strong for their children, and most of the time that's warranted. After all, you've been safeguarding your kids since they were born. That means the energy has always been flowing one way—from you to them. By demonstrating to them your shortcomings and your vulnerability, you are, for the first time, allowing a bit of that energy to flow back to you. And when you have shown them that you, too, need love, support, encouragement and, sometimes, even sympathy, you'll be creating the strong family bonds that are worth more than millions.

Now that your grown-up children know you are really human, it's time to broaden that impression and involve them further by sharing your goals with them. Where are you taking the business? Is your primary goal to increase sales to a higher figure, or is it to capture market share? Or is your main goal to produce the finest quality product in your industry? Sam Nomura, the real estate developer, is very clear to his kids about his goal. He wants to build one of the most beautifully-planned developments in California and make a profit at the same time. Sam's two sons are caught up in the challenge, and they're working hard at it. Sam is pleased that the three of them not only share this goal but, together, are setting new ones all the time.

Sharing your business and investment goals with your family means more than merely stating them. It means letting your children feel they are a part of the picture by telling them the risks involved and the challenges that must be overcome in order to meet your goals. It means listening to their opinions about the best way to reach those goals, and about the importance of the goals, themselves. And lastly, sharing your goals also means letting your children feel your excitement about the challenge of using wealth effectively and wisely.

The title of this chapter is "Introducing Your Business To Your Family," but you are actually doing more than that. You are also introducing your *business self* to your family. By sharing with your children how you got started, the problems you've overcome and the mistakes you've made, you are revealing a great deal about what makes you tick. No matter what else you do, this sharing of yourself will be one of the greatest legacies you can ever leave your children.

5 How Your Business Affects Your Family

You are probably the most influential role model your children will ever know. It would be hard to overestimate your effect on them, an effect that will last throughout their lives. Sherry X., the sole heiress to a chain of furniture stores, recalls her experience. "My parents often talked about values—that I should always be honest, never steal or cheat, and that I should heed the Golden Rule. As far as I could tell, when I was growing up, they were honest and formally polite—I mean, they never shouted or used bad language with the servants. But as I got older, I began to realize that they didn't really live their values.

"They hired furniture movers for six months and then fired them and rehired new people so they wouldn't have to pay wages of fifty cents more per hour. And when one of the movers got hurt from a heavy bed frame, they fought him in court to get out of paying for the part of the medical bills that the state didn't cover.[1]

"At home, Mom told me about the charities they were donating to, but then I watched my Mom call the maid to come from another part of the house to pick up something from the floor that my Mom could just have bent over and gotten herself. And when we were having a dinner party, Dad would make the cook stay late after she'd worked all day, even though Mom and Dad knew she had four small children at home to take care of.

"So I gradually started to realize that Mom and Dad weren't living the values they talked about. Oh, they never did anything illegal, but they were totally insensitive to the welfare of others.

After that, I stopped trusting them. To this day I still don't trust them. I mean, they're my Mom and Dad, and I love them and I appreciate what they've done for me, but I don't trust them. The worst thing about it is that once in a while, in spite of my knowing better, I find myself doing the same things they do, and then I just hate myself."[2]

Your children are generally more aware of the negative effects of role modeling than the positive ones. But the positive effects of role modeling can be a powerful influence as well. An acquaintance of mine in the publishing business tells this story about how his father affected him.

"I grew up in Chicago during the years of World War II. Things were scarce then, and food was rationed. But in the midst of these scarcities, our family was fortunate because my father had a wholesale food business and we were able to get just about everything edible. Everyone liked my dad—he had friends everywhere, and he knew how to treat them. I got a good glimpse of how that worked one day, as well as how the city of Chicago worked.

"That day I was riding in my dad's truck, helping to deliver some large wheels of hard-to-get Wisconsin cheddar cheese to some posh restaurants. The downtown section of Chicago known as 'The Loop' was, even then, a very crowded area. It was almost impossible to find a parking place. At that time, all of the downtown traffic police rode horses, and spent most of their time handing out parking tickets to the illegally parked cars and trucks. We double-parked our truck in front of a restaurant and, before making the delivery, my Dad took a big knife and cut a wedge out of one of the cheese wheels and wrapped it up. Those cheese wheels were really big—about 90 lbs. each—and that one wedge weighed almost 20 lbs. My Dad told me it was for one of the cops (that's what they called themselves—never 'policeman') who was having a hard time making ends meet.

"Moments later I heard the clip-clop of hooves on pavement, and a burly, middle-aged cop came up to our truck and leaned over into the cab. He called out, 'Hi, Carl, Hawaya? That your sonny boy with you?' I waved to the cop and, after the mutual inquiries about families were over, my Dad said, 'Mike, I'm overloaded with too much stuff this week, and it's only going to waste. I wonder if you could use it,' and he handed over that big wedge of cheese. The cop's eyes lit up over that, and he stuck the cheese into his saddlebag, two-thirds of it sticking out like a bright orange tower. After thanking my Dad, the cop asked, 'Delivering today, Carl?' My Dad told him yes and the cop said, 'Just double-park here and I'll watch things for you.' I helped my Dad carry in two cheese wheels and when we came back outside, there was the cop, seated on his tall, brown horse, holding up a line of traffic until my Dad could move our truck out of the way. That was how Chicago worked in those days. It wasn't exactly bribery or payoff—I sensed the cop would have helped my Dad even without the gift of cheese. And though I was just a young boy, I remember being impressed by my father's thoughtfulness, not only in giving, but in the way he had given so that the cop lost no dignity in receiving.

In all of his business dealings, my dad was a wonderful role model. Kindness, loyalty and respect for others flowed from him like water from a spring. And where most of us count ourselves fortunate to have a few really close friends, my Dad had them by the dozens—persons who would do anything for him, and vice versa. I've tried to do the same thing with my employees, with my associates and with my own son and daughter. I owe my Dad a large debt of gratitude, and I think of him often as I try to be as positive an influence on my children as he was to me."

Part of the role model you present to your children comes from your own self-image. And while your own self-image should be based on what you think of yourself as a whole person, often it is not. Some entrepreneurs have a self-image that is based on their net worth. When a self-image is based on possessions, that person may talk about himself in terms of how many houses he owns, and the value of his company and investments. With others, their self-image comes from their title as CEO. When self-image is based on a title, that individual will think of himself in terms of his role as money maker. With these kinds of self-images, you are saying to your children, "The more money I make, or the more possessions I own, the more important and powerful I am."

As your children grow up, they see the use of money and power as a way of solving problems. They observe how their parents use money to impact business, political and personal needs. From watching this over the years, they can easily assume that money and power are necessary in order to be important.

When your children become adults and see that your self-worth is based, for example, on your title as CEO, what happens to the young men and women who can't be CEO? They may end up feeling that they're not worth anything. This happened in Don Penning's family, where Don had three sons, and spent years telling them how great it was to be CEO, how owning and controlling your own company was the only way to go. Don was so wrapped up in his self-image as CEO that it never occurred to him what he was doing to his sons. He chose one of them to take over as CEO, and the other two sons elected to take jobs with other companies. Even though these young men have leadership ability and even though they're advancing as executives, they have to live with the constant feeling that they don't measure up. They know, from Dad, that being CEO is what counts, and that their brother has succeeded and they haven't.

The scope of role modeling covers every aspect of life. Who sees the affection between you and your wife, or the lack of it? Who watches how you treat relatives, friends, associates and even strangers? Who is aware of whether or not you bring integrity to your business deals? And who senses if you are fair or unfair, kind or cruel, honest or dishonest, generous or selfish? Your children notice all of this. And, by and large. they won't live the way you *tell* them to live—they'll live the way *you* live. Of all the assets you can leave your children, none is more precious than the role model you provide for them.

Another major factor in guiding your sons and daughters is to create a healthy relationship between them and the family wealth. This means understanding that wealth is a part of the family. And just as women give birth to children, entrepreneurs, both male and female, beget wealth. In the majority of cases, the entrepreneur sees the development of wealth in much the same way that a mother experiences the birth and growth of her children. In this sense, the wealth is a member of the family, and the children are brothers and sisters to it.

Most of us try to treat our sons and daughters with equal love and attention, and not play favorites. We realize that each child has his or her own strengths and weaknesses, but this is no reason to favor one over the other. So if the wealth is just one more brother or sister in the family, why does Dad lavish so much time and attention on it? It's because the wealth is the "kid" that gives the most back to Dad. He gets all of his strokes from it. And where we get our strokes is where we spend our time.

Does the rest of the family notice? You bet they do. They know who Dad's favorite "kid" is. Many wives look upon the business as a mistress. And the children have every right to react just like brothers and sisters do when they feel that their parents love one more than another.

It's natural for Dad to get so involved in the business that it eats up most of his time. But this sends the family a double message: Dad professes to love the family first, but what the kids see is, "My brother, the business, is what Dad loves most." And the moment you have that, your children start to get jealous of the business sibling who is getting all the attention. Some possible fallout of this is when the your daughter's actions say, "I couldn't get you to come my ballet recital, Dad, but I know I'll get your attention if I get pregnant." Or with your son's involvement with drugs: "You missed the basketball game again, Dad, but if I'm doing dope I'll bet you notice."

Most business owners with families have conflicting goals: spend time with the business or spend time with the family. The owner is frequently under stress because he always seems to be neglecting one for the other. I remember one of our clients—Phil Kronner—telling me how much he loved his wife and kids, and how important they were to him. I said, "Phil, you're telling me how important Jessie and the kids are to you, and yet you spend 90% of your time with the business and only 10% with them. Phil, something's out of balance."

Faced with a choice between business and family, many business owners opt for the business. Graduations are missed, family vacations get canceled, one-on-one time with the children is absent and the family hears a thousand excuses why Dad isn't there. Dad knows that he's been neglecting his children, and they know it too. Although it may not be expressed, the family knows that Dad loves—his business.

I once met a young lady on a plane. She had a darling baby that was just a few months old. I told her how excited I was with the birth of my grandsons, and I mentioned how excited her father must be about her bringing the baby home for him to see for the first time.

She said, "My father doesn't love the baby the way you are talking about. My father only loves with money. He bought the round-trip tickets for me to come, but I know he won't take the time to come to the airport." During the last 30 minutes of the flight, I begged her to share her feelings with her father, because he needed to hear her say that. He wouldn't like it, of course, but he needed to hear it. After we had left the plane, I followed behind her, still convinced that with a new baby, her father would come. I was sure he would be there with open arms. I waited quite a long time while she stood there with the baby and her luggage. When I finally had to leave, I walked over to her and asked her if she needed help in arranging transportation. With a sad little smile, she said, "No, the chauffeur will be here eventually."

This kind of perception, that Dad or Mom loves with money, is frequent among the grown-up children of wealthy families. A son or daughter will say to me that Dad, in particular, doesn't know how to hug or show affection, he only loves with money when he feels guilty. Interestingly, they don't say this critically—it's a statement of fact, an acceptance of the way things are.

But behind the buying off of his children is Dad's neglect of them. This doesn't come from an intentional desire to neglect them, it arises because it is difficult for Dad to communicate or share activities with them. Faced with this difficulty, Dad turns to business challenges, which though complex, *are emotionally easier for him to handle*. Because the business provides for the family, overcoming business challenges instills a sense of duty in Dad. He feels that by spending so much time with the business he is really doing it for the family. In fact, in many cases, Dad has rationalized away his lack of ability to communicate with his kids and to be with them. And because he is more respected and generally gets more strokes at the business than with the family, Dad's sense of esteem and accomplishment are reinforced through the business.

This isn't a chapter on psychology or on how to get your children to love you. It's purpose is to encourage you to develop a better balance between your business and your children. If your grown-up children are going to take over the running of the business or if they will be responsible to some degree for managing family wealth, someone has to start changing their perceptions of the role of the business and/or wealth in the family.

The essential requirement in bringing the role of the business into better balance is for Dad to spend more time with the family while the children are at home. The children need to know that the business need not be the all-demanding, all-consuming demon that steals all of Dad's time and energy. The family needs to know there is time for the kids, time for Mom, time to go camping, fishing, traveling or whatever they want to do together as a family. It doesn't have to be a lengthy trip. It may mean that, once in a while, Dad will spend an entire day with just one son or daughter.

This is an appropriate point to briefly mention the role of surrogate parents as part of the problem of imbalance. In her doctoral thesis, *The Experience of Inherited Wealth: A Social-Psychological Perspective,*[1] Joanie Bronfman reports on children of wealthy parents: "They described parents who were cold, distant, frequently absent, and who delegated much of the child-rearing to servants. These parents were often willing to relate to their children only on their own terms and they seemed more concerned that their children learned appropriate attitudes and behaviors than that they were well nurtured."

Only later, when hindsight brings lost opportunities into focus, do many entrepreneurs realize that they should have spent more time instilling values and building relations with their children.

Finding the appropriate balance between your business and your family is not easy, and it requires a certain amount of discipline, delegating authority and planning ahead. When you're finalizing the figures for the annual report, trying to figure out the real cause of production delays and dealing with a difficult employee lawsuit, it's hard to remember that your family needs your attention at home. It's a matter of priorities. But if you weren't already accomplished at juggling priorities, you'd never have been successful in business. What's needed, then, is to move your family up from the bottom of the list.

Part of your skill in running a business is verifying that you have met certain goals or standards, and correcting things when you have not. The same thing applies to finding the time to spend with your family. Keep a record of some kind to periodically see how you're doing. Have you fulfilled *all* of your promises to your family? Probably not, but you're still a beginner at this. Remember the story I told about beginners in the Introduction, about my trying to juggle silk scarves? As a beginner, you won't have a perfect record immediately— sometimes you'll fail. That's okay, but it's important to let your family know that you are trying, and that you want to work with them to rebuild their trust in you.

Ross Perot, Jr. expressed the idea well in Fortune Magazine, when he talked about his famous father: "Kids have to know you've made them your No.1 priority. Even when Dad was busy traveling around the country on business, he would fly back to see us if we were in a school play. He always made sure we knew how special we were to him."

Setting aside time for your children, and making that time inviolable, is one of the most effective ways to build family relationships and to instill positive values in your children. It is a high-yield investment.

1, 2   Bronfman, Joanie, Doctoral thesis, *The Experience Of Inherited Wealth: A Social-Psychological Perspective*, UMI Dissertation Service, Ann Arbor, MI, 1987

6 Creating Family Values

While you, as a role model, will strongly influence your children with your personal values, they will also gain values from their own unique perspective. This chapter is about your family members learning to share their personal values in order to discover common family values. It is about sharing personal goals in order to develop common family goals—goals to which each family member can contribute as part of the team.

This process begins with the most basic relationship of the family—your marriage. The experiences of the McDowell family provide an example of how the quality of the marriage affects the family.

Hugh McDowell's family looked every bit the successful American dream. Married for 20 years, with three healthy, attractive children, a beautiful home with a 50-acre ranch, and a thriving loan brokerage business that Hugh had built up over the years. There were two daughters and a son, in elementary and middle schools, and the children were about as well-behaved as children ought to be. Hugh and his wife, Emy, never fought and rarely disagreed. To all appearances, the McDowells lived in peace and harmony. They were wealthy, the kids seemed happy and were getting good grades in school, and both husband and wife seemed to be satisfied with their lives.

A closer look, however, showed that something was fundamentally wrong. Hugh spent most of his time at the office and, since Emy had domestic help at home, she was often absent as well, helping civic groups and the local theatrical association. In the few hours Hugh and Emy spent together at home, they didn't have much to say to each other or to the children. Hugh asked the kids a few obligatory questions about school and then ducked behind the newspaper.

Emy left meal preparation to the cook and, after making small talk with the children and formally kissing them, excused herself since she was needed at a theatrical staff meeting.

It was all very polite and restrained. The children returned to their rooms, where each one had his own TV, VCR and computer. They spent most of their time at home in their rooms, and seldom played with each other.

This had been going on for several years. Hugh and Emy had separate lives and had gradually ceased talking to each other. Now, they were on parallel tracks—sharing the house and some of the routine of a family—while those tracks moved on, never coming together. In fact, there was no real family. Hugh and Emy and the children had become roomers in a luxurious boarding house, each person seeking his own, private agenda.

Hugh first realized that something had to change when he began to think about a succession plan and a possible role for his children. After I had been chosen as facilitator, and we had had our first family meeting, it was obvious to me that a good deal of work on sharing needed to be done before tackling the problems of succession. After the meeting, I met privately with Hugh in order to ask some blunt, personal questions. I started with, "Why are you married? I don't want to know why you originally got married, I want to know why you are married today."

I didn't expect a quick answer, and it was a few months before we met again to discuss it. Hugh said he had thought about it quite a bit but had no simple answer. I explained to Hugh that *marital trust and sharing* is essential in order to have *family trust and sharing*. I then suggested that he and Emy do something they had not done for many years—go away together and spend an entire weekend or more to try to understand why they were married, and if there were sufficient reasons for them to continue to be married. It took some convincing, but they finally did it.

They stayed together for four days in a lodge at a beautiful resort area. Going along with my request, they agreed to remain in their room or take walks together—no distracting activities—until they had come up with some answers. Those days were filled with strong emotions, some fierce fights and not a few tears. In their particular case, Hugh and Emy's passive, mutual withdrawal had been precipitated by a marital problem that had erupted years before and had been swept under the rug. Over the years, they had deliberately built walls around themselves—walls that had prompted the children to emulate them by building their own walls.

During this intense weekend, Hugh and Emy were jolted out of their complacent separateness, and forced to look at themselves anew. What they saw made them both agree that their marriage had a lot worth saving. They also agreed that there was much work to be done, and they committed themselves to tearing down the walls of separation.

A while later, at my suggestion, the McDowells agreed to a vacation that was unlike anything they'd ever done before. The idea was to make a certain amount of time and money available and, with as few restrictions as possible, let the children plan the vacation on their own. This meant deciding where to go, how to get there, arranging for travel tickets, tours and guides where necessary; changing money, researching weather conditions at their destination, and arranging for any required visas. It was a most extraordinary trip. Everyone did some things for the first time: Mom climbed her first mountain; Dad, for the first time in his marriage, sat back and allowed his wife and children to tell him what to do; and the children did everything from ordering meals in foreign languages to zooming down a bobsled run (with experienced guides) at 60 miles per hour.

The vacation was an enormous success. When he told me about it after they had returned, Hugh was so proud of the competence his youngsters had exhibited that he was about to burst. He and Emy had spent countless lunches, chatting about things that interested them both. At the next family board meeting, it was like seeing a different family. For the first time in years, they had begun to *like* each other.

Hugh's and Emy's marriage began to improve from that time on, and the quality of their relationship had a powerful, beneficial effect on their children. Although they didn't see the connection at first, their improved marriage was the necessary first step on the road to the eventual, effective transfer of wealth. This is because the plans for transfer of wealth begin with basics, and the basics are the milestones of learning to communicate, to share, to raise the level of mutual trust, to develop teamwork and, finally, to express the affection and love that enables a group of individuals to become a real family.

If you're not communicating, sharing and expressing affection with your spouse on a daily basis, what you *are* doing is providing a negative role model for your children. A part of their growing up to become responsible, competent and healthy adults is to be given the experience of watching their Dad and Mom exhibit not only intelligence and competence, but affection, intimacy and love. After looking closely at why they are married, some of my clients have decided to separate. After a period of intense and sincere communication, where partners take a close look at themselves and their lives, the marriage either gets better or it dissolves—it rarely remains the same. The reasons for remaining together are varied, and often include not only love for each other and concern for children, but comfort, convenience, mutual support, valuing shared experiences, and so on. On the other side, I had one client where the husband and wife decided there really was no basis for continuing their marriage.

Typically, in the wealthy entrepreneurial family, dad has been off creating the business and interacting with the world on a daily basis, while mom has been charged with domestic responsibilities and charitable work. This makes for vastly different experiences which require very different skills. The effect of these different daily experiences sometimes causes the entrepreneur to feel he has outgrown his spouse, and that there is no longer a basis for sharing (unfair, though that may be). Conversely, the spouse's exposure to a diversity of culture may make her feel that her husband's interests have remained narrow.

Different daily routines do not, of course, necessarily lead to incompatible partners. But busy entrepreneurs. whether male or female, often tend to avoid discussing their changing outlook with their spouse. If one partner's values and interests change while their partner's remain static, after a while there is simply no basis for sharing. One-sided growth like this usually creates a lot of animosity and, sometimes, a difficult divorce.

Although values which have to do with women's careers and domestic duties have changed rapidly over the past decades in the general population, in the wealthy, entrepreneurial family, mom often has some special burdens imposed on her. Although she is free from having to worry about finding the money to pay bills, and although she may have domestic help in running the home, the wealthy mom is expected to maintain a certain image. She is expected to remain lean and attractive, and to always dress "right." She must know how to entertain properly, and she is expected to do volunteer work on a regular basis. In general, wealthy moms are discouraged from pursuing careers of their own. Their value to the family is measured, in many cases, by how well they reflect on their husband and whether or not they produce quality heirs.[1]

Accepting your spouse and children for themselves is not always easy. Jordan and Margaret Paul give one reason why: "Have you ever wondered why grandparents are more loving with their grandchildren than they were with their own children? Have you noticed yourself being more accepting of other people's children than of you own? Nothing touches us as deeply as our family relationships. The more important the relationship, the more our fears and learned childhood reactions become activated. And we become unloving. We find it hardest to give love to those who need our love the most—our immediate family."[2]

One of the effects of poor communication is that the love which does exist between family members is almost never expressed. If you, as entrepreneur. love your wife and your children, but never tell them, they may not know it. If you don't express your affection for them with hugging and other touching, as well as with kind words, they may not believe it even if you say it. Among the families of our clients, my staff and I are finding more and more feelings of isolation, alienation and abandonment. So if you really love your family, you have to find some ways to express that love to them other than just through money.

It's often hard for a person who has been an entrepreneur for many years to express love. After all, love is giving of yourself unconditionally, with no strings attached and no judgments, loving that person whatever he or she is. What makes this hard for entrepreneurs is that so many of their business relationships are based on performance—I will admire and reward you based on how you perform for me. I have a client—Noel Mandell--who is a rice grower...has about 2000 acres planted. Noel was estranged from his daughter for years. He wanted her to get an MBA and manage his agribusiness, but Catherine—he calls her Cat—got this idea to start her own printed circuit factory across the Mexican border near San Diego.

He hadn't seen her for three years and he was very unforgiving. He said to me, "Roy, she's doing it all wrong. I told her to get her education first but she just wouldn't listen." I told him that Cat was getting her PhD in the school of hard knocks, which for her may be a better way to learn. But Noel was really stubborn. His daughter wasn't performing to his standards. That year, when Christmas came, I said to him, "Why don't you go down and see Cat? That's what you really want to do, isn't it?" He admitted it was, so I said, "Why don't you get in an airplane and go?" Noel said, "I can't get reservations now, during Christmas, they're all booked." So I said, "So what? Rent a plane. What is it going to cost you, ten thousand dollars? Big deal. Call up the airport, charter a plane and go down there. What difference is ten thousand going to make to you?" Noel said, "Well, let me think about it." That usually means "no," but in this case, he did it. And he not only did it, he took his wife and his other daughter and her husband with him. They spent a week in Costa Rica with Cat. It was the greatest week he had ever spent in his adult life. This was the first time he had ever gone somewhere without an agenda. One day, he spent six hours, reading in a hammock. It was the most restful vacation of his life. Most important of all, Noel realized that all his years of judging his daughter had kept him estranged from her—that the problem had been his.

When we talked about it after he came back, it became clear that Noel had had a lot of fear about love. He was a man who drove himself hard and rarely gave himself credit for his accomplishments. No matter how successful he was, he knocked holes in his self-image. And that was a big part of his problem. Because he couldn't accept himself, couldn't love himself, neither could he really accept or love others.

After a lot of soul-searching, Noel is finally learning that allowing himself to be vulnerable is not a weakness but a strength. Another way of putting it is that he's learning to cast out fear—fear of failure, fear of not measuring up, fear that others won't measure up. This has done wonders for his relationship with his daughter. Now he accepts her, accepts her decisions—he even asks her advice now and then, which is really something for Noel.

Love is very important to me in my work and in my personal life. I see it as the basis for everything we do and everything we hope to accomplish. I think it's really that way for everyone—at least that's my instinct. The problem is not so much the absence of love as much as the lack of communication of it. When people stop communicating, stop talking to each other with sincerity...or when talking becomes just a superficial exchange of words, that's when love seems to dry up. That's why, throughout this book, I keep emphasizing the importance of communication.

One way to show and receive love, without words, is through hugging. Another of my clients—Al Luder—was the kind of guy who might hug a woman, but never a man. After one family meeting...it was after the evening dinner, and we were all standing around in the restaurant foyer. I gave Mom and the daughters and the son a hug, and Dad disappeared. I never did find him. A couple of weeks later, when I was talking to him on the phone, I said, "Al, you know you ran off the other night?" He started to laugh, and I said, "You couldn't handle that hugging, could you?" He said, "Roy, you have to understand, I get very uncomfortable with that. I was not raised with hugging men." I told Al, "You're not going to get away with that—you know you're going to get hugged next time." Al said, "I know—I'm preparing myself."

After the next family board meeting with the Luders, I gave him a hug and said, "Now, was that so bad?" Al replied, "It's not that it's so bad, it just makes me very uncomfortable." Al couldn't change overnight. It took two years for him to be comfortable with hugging and touching. But the great news is that, after that board meeting, Al hugged his son for the first time. You could just see the distance between them melting. It was wonderful.

After, that first hug, Al and his son began to do more things together. Since they were both interested in track and field events, they went together to several track meets, and they rediscovered that they both liked chess. In fact, as with most families, Al Luder's family found out that they all shared many values. At a family board meeting we went through an exercise of listing basic values (the Five Equities, which I describe in the next Chapter). The evening was filled with "ah-hah's" from both the parents and their children, and expressions like, "Gee, I didn't realize you also thought that way."

Of course, each individual family member is going to have some different ideas—and that's okay. But one of the real satisfactions which comes from family communication is to see that your children, and your grandchildren, in their own time, have absorbed the basic values of life that you hold in high regard.

Two closely-related fundamental values which make a family work are integrity, and its result—trust. Unfortunately, it's not uncommon for these to be absent between parents and children. Often, dad, as entrepreneur, holds high ethical standards in business. His "word" means something among his associates—when he gives it, he keeps it, and they all know it and can depend on it. If dad hadn't been keeping his promises in his business dealings, he would never have become so successful.

So it's strange to see dad's integrity in family dealings fall short of his proclaimed standards. This most often happens in "little" things—that is, things that are little to dad but not to the children. When dad says he'll be home at 4:00 p.m. to watch his son's tennis match, will he make the same effort to be on time as he does for a business conference? Will dad be late, or will he call home that day to say that some "important" business problem has come up and he won't be able to make it?

"Little" things. Like when dad says he'll stop and pick up the corsage for his daughter's dance, and then forgets all about it. (Somehow, he never forgets to bring his notes to a business conference.) Whether or not dad keeps his word on promises to the family determines, for them, his level of integrity and the degree of trust with which he is viewed. He may have a reputation as a dependable, square-dealing businessman and still fail miserably at home.

Dad's own behavior, in relation to what he says, is also closely watched by the children, even if it is not expressed. When dad preaches to his boys about never drinking and driving, and they see him come home intoxicated, their trust in him is demolished. After watching this kind of behavior, the children think, "What you do is so loud I can't hear what you say," and they simply stop listening.

It is important for dad to follow through on family commitments and to live up to what he preaches to the children. Dad has no more justification for reneging on a deal with the family than he does with the business. This is the basis for family trust.

Without trust, there is no basis for communication, whether it is between husband and wife, parents and children, business partners or even between countries. Trust is a sacred gift one gives and receives, based upon merit, and it can also be taken away quickly. How do you gain trust and how do you decide when to give your trust? If a son or daughter makes a mistake with money and gets into debt, or irresponsibly gets into an auto accident, the parents will often withdraw their trust and start to feel that their child is not trustworthy in other areas as well.

When I work with families on the issue of trust, we look at the three roots of trust: competence, reliability and sincerity. From these, we can begin to see where we may be placing trust erroneously or where we may be withholding trust to our own and others' detriment.

To illustrate this point, let's use the example of a client who gave his grown-up daughter $35,000 because she was in debt and had no way to get out. With the $35,000 in cash, instead of paying off the debt, she put a down payment on a boat, thereby creating more debt. Her father was outraged, and screamed that she was stupid and irresponsible and could not be trusted with anything. He had made an extremely broad generalization from just this one instance.

But the situation looks different when we examine it more closely. The daughter had had no training or experience whatsoever in dealing with money. On the contrary, she had been sheltered all of her life—all of her bills had been paid for her and, to a large degree, she had had access to unlimited funds. In addition, she had previously not fulfilled many of her promises about using money. Therefore, she had no record of competence or reliability in dealing with money. So while her father knew she was sincere when she had needed the money (that what she had told him was the truth), he also knew she was neither competent nor reliable. Two of the three elements of trust were absent. When he gave her the $35,000, he was really setting her up for failure. How much better off they both would have been if he had acknowledged that his daughter could not yet be trusted with money, and had given her some assistance to become more competent. In this way, they would both have grown from the experience.

Time and time again I see situations in families, where the lack of competence or reliability is well known, but parents still continue to give their grown-up children and their spouses responsibilities they are unprepared for and cannot fulfill. The same thing is true when parents know their son or daughter is insincere but they place responsibilities on him or her in spite of it.

The key to building trust is to understand the necessity for sincerity, competence and reliability all to be present. If they do not exist together, we are being unfair to ourselves and to others when we expect a certain level of performance from them. By being aware of the absence of either sincerity, competence or reliability in our grown-up children, spouses, employees or others, we can offer the kind of help that will enable them to accept greater and greater challenges, to become trustworthy. And by so doing, we will eliminate a lot of conflict.

It is important to understand that trustworthiness is not a static, permanent state, it is a temporary assessment that can change. We shouldn't assume that someone can never be deserving of our trust. While we begin by assessing a person's sincerity, competence and reliability, and thus the level of our trust, we can then move to the next step: what kind of coaching or other assistance do they need to improve? Can we communicate their need to improve in a constructive way that will help them want to improve? If I tell someone, "I don't trust you," that's the end of the discussion. But if I say to that person: "For me to be able to increase my trust in you, I need to see you improve in the area of reliability. I'm willing to help you do that if you're willing to try." That leaves room for change, and the possibility that trust will be enhanced.

Trust among family members is a prerequisite not only for good communication but for learning to work as a team. With trust, there is room to develop mutual understanding. Within the family, you start to learn about each other, what each person's skills are, what each has to offer, and how to deal with an individual's weak points. Maybe there is one individual that the rest of the family tends to discount all the time, and they focus on his weaknesses rather than on his strengths. Maybe, when he has an idea, he doesn't think it through all the way. That doesn't mean his idea is no good, it just means that the family needs to ask him a lot more questions to see if the idea is really valid. When the family looks carefully at the merits of an idea, regardless of who thought of the idea, that's good communication. When the family learns to make use of everyone's skills, allowing each person to contribute to the extent of their ability, that's real teamwork.

With family members beginning to trust and respect each other, and to work as a team, they're ready for the next step: developing family goals. Why are family goals needed? Drs. Jordan and Margaret Paul, give a good reason in their book on parent-child relations.

"An old Chinese proverb states: 'If we do not change our direction, we are likely to end up where we are headed.' The application for families is clear: parents need to take the time to reflect on goals for their families. No one would think of running a business without setting goals, but amazingly few parents take the time to do this for their families."[2]

Family goals depend a lot on each individual's view of happiness and success. Is success to be measured in monetary terms, by degree of education, by the number of awards received, or by how much good has been done for the world? Is happiness to be defined as lack of anxieties, as comfort, as self-acceptance or as joy and enthusiasm? A facilitator is of real help here, because the siblings often don't know what they mean by happiness and success. Money and objects have too frequently been the only measuring stick.

For several years, this was a problem for the Hansen family. Leonard Hansen was extremely successful in business. He manufactured machine tools, and his sales were somewhere around 70 million. Len had an amazing art collection—one of the finest private collections of Renaissance paintings in the U.S. Len and his wife, Gail, got so wrapped up in their art collection that it seemed to take over their lives. Family happiness and success were determined by how many art pieces they owned, as well as their value.

Between the business and the art collection, the Hansens had no time for their children, and nannies became the mentors. The parents were mostly absent, on long trips, to add to the collection. When they were home, there were endless social gatherings within the art world. Meanwhile, the kids were growing up strangers to their parents.

It took the Hansens a long time to realize that they'd gotten hooked by the possession of things and by status. Now, when the children are in their late teens and are getting ready to leave home, Dad and Mom have belatedly realized that their children are more important than their collection. It's still possible to overcome the years of neglect but it will be costly in terms of time, energy and expense.

The issue is whether success is going to be measured by material things, or by how family members feel about themselves. One of the initial objectives of the family getting together in periodic board meetings is to see if all family members can find some common elements in their definitions of success and happiness. If your family can't agree on what constitutes success and happiness, it's difficult to develop many common goals.

There are some basic questions that have to be answered before family goals can emerge. For example, what is the family? Is it mom and dad and the kids? Does it include the spouses of the grown-up children? Does it include the grandchildren? How about step-brothers and step-sisters? What do we mean by long term? The Iroquois Indians think in terms of seven generations. Some Asian cultures think in terms of hundreds of years. In the U.S., it's a rare family that thinks and plans beyond the first generation.

In the next chapter, we'll look more closely at the meaning of happiness, success and fulfillment, and how your family can begin to identify goals through the Five Equities.

1   Bronfman, Joanie, Doctoral thesis, *The Experience Of Inherited Wealth: A Social-Psychological Perspective,* UMI Dissertation Service, Ann Arbor, MI, 1987

2   Paul, Jordan and Margaret, *If You Really Loved Me,* Compcare Publishers, Minneapolis, MN, 1987

7 Feelings, Values and Goals

A very close friend of mine shared with me an intimate story about feelings. When he was forty years old, someone asked him, "How do you feel about that?" His replies all concerned how he *thought* about the subject. But the questioner wanted to know if he felt frustrated, sad, exhilarated, etc. As my friend pondered the question over the next few months, he realized that he had never consciously acknowledged a feeling in his life. His new-found insight was the beginning of a magical transformation from brain to heart, and an awareness of a world he had long ago buried.

Feelings, although sometimes painful, are wonderfully true indicators of what's really going on inside of us. They can be accurate and/or trigger things we learned as children which can be destructive. So, awareness and acknowledgement of them is important. When we repress or ignore them, they remain inside us as hidden manipulators, compelling us to action or inaction that is not in our interest and, often, filling us with anguish.

It has been my experience that when we are divorced from our feelings, it's easy to go astray. I see that happening in many of our institutions. In our legal system, for example, lawyers and judges are fond of saying we are "a nation of laws and not of men." What this suggests, of course, is that laws protect us from the tyranny of unrighteous acts. Yet almost everyone who has been involved with legal matters knows that laws can be manipulated for unethical purposes.

I was recently in the offices of a well-known lawyer, and two of the partners and I were talking about the legal system. After some time, I asked this question: "Where does justice fit into the system?" They were silent for a moment, with incredulous looks on their faces. One of them said, "What do you mean, 'justice?' That term never enters into the conversation in this law firm. The only issue is to win or lose. And you had better win. Period!"

When the law becomes depersonalized, the victims are not only the litigants, but the principles of everyone involved. An acquaintance of mine illustrates this with the following true story.

"I was driving through the city of Oakland a few months ago, and I witnessed a terrible accident. An elderly woman drove through a red light in a busy intersection. She didn't notice a motorcycle crossing the intersection. I watched in horror as the motorcycle and rider rammed into the side of her car. The rider was thrown into the air and landed some twenty feet away on the pavement. He was wearing a helmet, but the impact was so severe he lay unmoving, his legs twisted into a grotesque position.

"After he had been carried into an ambulance and taken away, I and several other witnesses described the accident to the police. A few days later I made inquiries and found out that the young man had survived—barely—with a broken back and pelvis, multiple fractures of his legs and serious internal injuries. His lower body would be completely paralyzed, with no chance of his ever regaining use of it. I learned that he was twenty three years old, married, with two toddlers. He had been an auto mechanic.

"I heard nothing more about the accident for two months, and I assumed all claims were being settled without my being called as a witness. But one morning, an insurance investigator came to see me.

"He was representing the woman driver's insurance company. She had claimed that the motorcycle driver was at fault, and the investigator had come to see if he could get a witness to corroborate her story so they could get a judgment against the young man.

"I asked him about the latest news of the young man's condition. He told me the medical report stated that he was permanently paralyzed and had undergone a dozen or more operations. He would probably not be released from the hospital for another six months. I asked if the woman who was the cause of the accident had been to see him, or his wife. The investigator replied, 'No, we strongly discourage any contact with opposing claimants.' A few minutes later, he left.

"That really bothered me. I suppose there is some merit in keeping insurance claimants apart after an accident—after all, the injured party might try to murder the other one. But it seems to me the system shielded her from any responsibility for her actions. She didn't have to face what she had done—it was simply a legal matter, to be handled by legal experts.

"But what would have happened if that woman had seen firsthand the pain inflicted on the young man; if she had seen the face of his young wife at the hospital, day after day, for months; if she had seen the little children and realized that she had forever deprived them of a normal father—*if she had seen any of that, and if she had any feelings, could she have allowed her insurance company to try to place the blame on him?*"

Each of us has probably heard some variation on this theme. The principle is that we know, we *feel*, that we have a responsibility to our neighbor; but the law says, no, we don't have a responsibility to our neighbor—we have a responsibility to follow our lawyer's advice. We don't go talk to the injured person and we don't apologize or try to make amends. We have been seduced into accepting a rational argument (let the lawyers handle it) in place of human decency.

An interesting example of moral vs. rational argument is in the experience of Anatoly Sharansky, the Russian dissident, who speaks of his years spent as a prisoner in a Soviet gulag.[1] The gulag officers and guards constantly tried to justify their own behavior and break the spirit of the prisoners by trying to convince them why their incarceration and harsh treatment were justified. They used all manner of arguments to do this: the prisoners were the parasites of society, all they wanted was disorder and chaos, they were scum who did not appreciate all the Soviet Union had done for them, and so on.

Sharansky's captors had all the advantages. In addition to weapons, they had good food, good health, warm clothing, news of the outside world and the ability to punish prisoners indiscriminately, which they did. Many of the inmates succumbed, and others, in order to get a scrap of food or a piece of clothing to avoid frostbite, admitted that they were indeed guilty and deserving of punishment.

Sharansky watched the KGB break the spirit of his fellow prisoners. When this happened, they began to weaken and die—their will to live had been broken. He felt his only strength, his only advantage was to cling to his moral sense of right and wrong. The KGB, with their gulags and tormentor guards, were wrong. There was only one way to survive. Sharansky recounts: "I had to remind myself that the basic rule of the game is that moral principle is much stronger than any rational argument."

Your values are the bedrock of your morals and ethics. Although you may intellectually understand that following the Golden Rule is the proper way for you to live, in practice, it is your values which ultimately guide you. When you see someone being wrongfully hurt, it is your underlying values that make you want to help, not your reasoning. This is what causes an otherwise unassuming person to spontaneously jump into a river to save a drowning child.

The Kronner family used to be an example of non-expression of values. I first mentioned the Kronners in Chapter 2, and how they never told their college-age children anything about family finances. In fact, there was not much communication, in general, between parents and children.

Phil and Jessie Kroner have been involved in charitable projects for many years, but their orientation has been on the amount of dollars spent each year for "charitable purposes." Their desire to give to charities—while heartfelt—has been expressed as an abstract principle, and they haven't been involved with the actual people who were overseeing the projects or with those who were receiving the benefits. Consequently, their children have grown up to think of charitable work as a numbers game rather than issues affecting real people. But last year, Phil and Jessie funded a group that was working in the Sahel region of North Africa, where they're always having trouble with drought. And without telling anyone, their son, Kevin, who was studying mechanical engineering in college, designed and tested a new ultra-simple, bicycle-powered water pump for use in developing countries. It was a neat gadget--it requires only about $25 dollars worth of parts for the whole thing, plus the use of a local bicycle.

Kevin got together with his sister, Julie, and together they created a proposal to manufacture the parts and make kits available. When they presented their proposal to their parents, they did it with such enthusiasm that Mom and Dad got all excited, too, and wanted to fund the project and get it going immediately. The kids agreed, and, two months later, a contract was signed to make prototypes, develop an on-site test program and, within a year, manufacture the parts for several thousand units.

This was the first time the Kronner family worked together on anything and it was probably the first time they had ever shared their feelings. One day, when the project was getting underway, Phil took his son and daughter aside and said to them, "I'm just so proud of both of you that I really don't know what to say." That was the first time the kids ever saw tears in their Dad's eyes. It was a whole new experience for all of them.

When it comes to helping family members to express values and feelings, one of the best tools of communication we at The Williams Group have devised is the Family Advisory Board, which I described in Chapter 2. The formal proceedings of these family meetings, the rules which prevent emotional scarring and the presence of a skilled facilitator all work to make the Family Advisory Board a safe and effective way for family members to express themselves. Another very effective tool for expressing and sharing deeply-held feelings is a system called the Five Equities.[2] Here's how it works:

All family members are asked to identify their personal values in five areas: spiritual, intellectual, psychological, physical and financial. We call these personal values equities because, like other assets, they can be very beneficial if clearly understood. For example, if your values about your physical condition are vague, it will be harder for you to maintain good health and vitality. If your values about your physical condition are clearly identified, they will aid you in reaching your goals.

Personal goals spring from personal values. Again using the example of physical condition, if I believe that it is good to have a healthy, vital and attractive body, then one of my goals will be to arrive at and maintain that kind of physical condition. With that goal in mind, I can formulate the specific steps I will need to undertake in order to get there and stay there.

There are two reasons for going through this procedure. The first is that we all occasionally need to look at our own lives to see if our goals really reflect our values, and if we are moving toward those goals on schedule. Secondly, sharing personal values and goals among family members provides a comfortable setting for each family member to share important things that do not usually get expressed.

The Five Equities chart that follows shows an example of what the values and goals might be for one individual. Of course, each person will have his or her own, individual set of values and goals. The process begins with a self-query to identify personal values—what I call governing values—are for each of the five categories. Once you have identified your governing values, they will suggest long-term goals.

For example, in the Intellectual category, if your governing values are to use your intellect to its fullest possible extent and to develop a broad knowledge base, this suggests that your long-term goal, for example, might be to go back to school and earn a degree in the humanities. From that long-term goal, your intermediate goal, over the next two years, might be to take courses that apply to that degree program. To help you get to your intermediate goal, you might commit yourself to a diverse reading program where you read a minimum amount each day. The point is that to uphold and obtain your life values, you need to support them by the things you do each day, and by your intermediate and long-term goals.

It's a good idea to frequently review your daily activities to make sure you are actually doing those activities that will lead to your longer-term goals. The Five Equities chart reminds you of those necessary daily activities and helps to keep you on track.

The Five Equities

Five Equities	Spiritual	Intellectual	Psycho-logical	Physical	Financial
Govern-ing Values:	There is a power and an intelligence greater than ourselves. It manifests as love.	Knowledge is beneficial, both for myself and for everyone else. I should develop my intellect to the greatest degree possible.	Self-love is a prerequisite to loving others. Maintain high principles.	Good health, vitality and energy. Bodies should be capable and attractive.	Money allows freedom, security, pleasure and the ability to help others.
Goals Long Term:	Be filled with unconditional love. Know the purpose of my life.	To be able to use knowledge to help others. To put my knowledge to good use.	Total self-acceptance and acceptance of others. Be a good friend.	Maintain health, attractiveness and vitality to old age.	Continue to build family wealth and use it responsibly.
Goals Next Two Years:	Be more content and more loving. Spread happiness to others.	Gain more knowledge of people. Learn more about what motivates others.	Learn to like myself more. Gain more empathy. Keep up friendships.	Stabilize my weight at 195 lbs. Maintain a healthy diet and exercise schedule.	Be able to have a basic under-standing of economics and finance, and the basics of stocks, bonds and insurance.
Goals Daily:	Spend some time each day in meditation and prayer. Do several good deeds each day.	Become a better listener, write observa-tions in daily journal.	Use daily reminder to tell myself I'm okay. Call/write friends.	30 minutes of aerobics each day. Do breath-ing and imaging exercises each day.	Design a daily reading and educational program, stick to it and not neglect it.

Your values and your goals are not set in concrete; you'll change them as you, yourself, change. But regardless of how you change, the Five Equities process will provide a path from the activities you do on a daily basis, to the ideal of actually living your personal values. It is a method for staying on track.

The Governing Values for Spiritual Equity

Most human beings have an inherent need for spirituality—a built-in striving to seek meaning and purpose for their lives, and to have a relationship with the Creator. This need assumes that there is some spiritual agency or force that is more good, more knowing and more powerful than ourselves. Your governing values for spiritual equity might include, for example, faith in God; the importance of love and compassion; the search for meaning; and the purpose of your time on earth.

The Governing Values for Intellectual Equity

Your intellectual equity is your personal store of knowledge, experience and skills. The governing values for intellectual equity may include creativity; love of learning; the benefits of knowledge; using your mind to its fullest extent; and the acquisition of wisdom. In fact, a possible governing value for intellectual equity is the idea that the purpose of being alive is to learn.

The Governing Values for Psychological Equity

What are the most important things to you about character, personality and relationships? Some governing values might have to do with yourself, such as integrity, self-acceptance, and maintaining your principles. Or they might include relationships with others, such as friendship, caring and trustworthiness.

The Governing Values for Physical Equity

What should your body be like? What should it be able to do? What is your ideal for good physical condition? The governing values for physical equity might include health, strength, vitality, agility, and grace or beauty. Together, these physical equity values can result in growing older more slowly.

The Governing Values for Financial Equity

The governing values for financial equity might include the importance of wealth to you; the purpose of wealth; and the acquisition of independence, freedom, power or luxury. Is the way in which you acquire money a part of your values?

When you look at the sample chart, notice that the values and goals are congruent—that is, the governing values determine the long-term goals; the long-term goals determine the two-year goals, etc. The process is *always done from top to bottom*, starting with governing values and ending with daily goals. This insures that what you start doing on a daily basis will eventually take you to your long-term goals and, when your long-term goals are fulfilled, you are living your fundamental life values.

There are two separate and distinct parts to the process of using the Five Equities: the first part is for the purpose of more clearly identifying and developing your own values and goals. This is a private procedure, done by you (and also done privately, by other members of your family). The second part is the sharing of your personal values and goals with other members of the family. This latter part is never forced upon anyone, but it is an extremely powerful method which provides insight into individual values and needs.

The second part of the Five Equities process—the sharing of values and goals—is where dramatic changes frequently happen. For what may be the first time in their lives, Mom and Dad are hearing their kids talk about things that are very important to them, things they've never had the opportunity to express. And on the other side, the kids, by hearing about the values and goals of Mom and Dad, start to better understand why Dad is involved with the business and what it means to the family. This is powerful stuff. In a safe atmosphere, free of the fear of being attacked or ridiculed, all family members are baring their souls to each other.

In Russ Lackland's family, going through the Five Equities caused a real breakthrough. Russ's son, James, the oldest of three boys, was being groomed to become president of the family business which is a land title company. Ever since James started college, everyone in the family assumed that he would be president—the subject was never even discussed. In fact, James didn't want to be president but he couldn't stand up to his strong-willed father and tell him so outright.

After all the Lacklands had completed their Five Equities sheets, we held a family board meeting. I had met privately with individual family members prior to the meeting, and I was able to assure the children that it would be absolutely safe for them to express their innermost feelings. I had also told Russ that his son had something important to express to him, and that it was crucial that he allow the boy the space to say what he wanted. During the meeting, each person shared his or her values and goals with the rest of the family.

There are always surprises when family members share like this for the first time, and the Lacklands learned much about each other that they hadn't known. But when it was James' turn, and he quietly read off what he had put down on his sheet, there was dead silence in the room. It was immediately apparent that this young man had no interest in being president. In fact, he had no interest in business at all. The information from his Five Equities showed that he was strongly drawn to spiritual values. After sharing his values and goals, James looked at me for support, then turned to his father and said, "Dad, I want to go to a seminary and become a minister." It took Russ Lackland some time to come to grips with this, but, of course, he did. And in the process he started to pay more attention to his other sons, and how they might or might not fit into the business.

When you share your deepest feelings with others in an atmosphere of mutual respect, whether you've known them a short time or all your life, a new kind of bond is created. It's as though, for the first time, all of the masks we wear have been removed, and we see the real human being—unique, individual and precious. The sharing of their deepest feelings was a real turnaround for the Lacklands. Dad and Mom began to listen to their sons and to see that their opinions were valid. Their sons, in turn, realized that their parents weren't mechanical authority figures, but were real people, with real feelings and problems and needs.

The Five Equities process is an effective tool, both for self-revelation and for bringing your family closer together. I cannot recommend it highly enough.

1   *Sharansky In SF: Games Yes, But Not With The KGB*, San Francisco Examiner, February 1, 1987

2   The Five Equities system, Alan Boal, Idea Transfer, Inc., San Clemente, California

8 When the Children Are Young

In Fortune Magazine, billionaire H. Ross Perot tells about the day, many years ago, when a reporter was interviewing him and his small son, Ross Jr., walked into his office. "So, young man," the reporter said, "how does it feel to be the son of the richest man in Texas?" "Mister," replied the boy, "all I know is I get twenty-five cents a week."[1]

It's an engaging thought, isn't it? A billionaire's son getting only twenty-five cents a week. Most people who hear this story feel good about it because it's demonstrating several sound principles. It tells us that the boy certainly wasn't being spoiled just because his family was rich, and that he was learning the discipline of money by receiving a regular, modest allowance. It also tells us that his parents were wise enough to begin his training at an early age.

This story about Ross Perot Jr. contrasts with other true stories about children in families of wealth, where parental absence, neglect and inattention are more common. In one instance a man recalls of his childhood, "I kept hurting myself. I had these little accidents—crashes. I had this little scooter and I kept falling off it and riding it into barbed wire fences. I was always trying to do myself in (so that) I could get attention from my Mom. Mom came running down and picked me up...and was around serving me and helping me. It was great."[2]

Another man remembers from his childhood: "We were lonely. It was disappointing when my father would take off a lot for business. That definitely contributed to a lack of close relationships. One thing that was tough was my parents would go away for a vacation and leave us with a nurse. But, of course, she could never substitute for Mom and Dad. This became sort of an unwitting weapon that they would use against us, their going away. We were never physically beaten up but we always would feel that when they would go away they were punishing us somehow."[3]

Often, in the absence of parental attention, a nanny takes on the role of mentor to the children. One of the problems with this is that the nanny, although well-intentioned, may have entirely different values than do the parents. Then, as the children grow up reflecting the values of their nanny, strong conflicts may arise between the values of the children and those of the parents. It's like rolling the dice—are you willing to take this kind of risk with your children?

In contrast to parental neglect when the children are young, some entrepreneurial dads who are used to dominating their business, dominate their children as well. This is what happened with Porter Scudder and his only son, Miles. Porter had built up a good-sized commercial bank by a combination of skill and tenacity. He was single-minded and never let anything get in his way for long. He was also single-minded about raising his son. He wanted Miles to fill his shoes as president of the bank—there was to be no question about it. By the time Miles was five years old, his father had so dominated the little boy that he had lost all initiative. By the time the boy was a teenager, he had lost any natural decision-making ability he might have had.

The terrible irony of this is that Porter, by so rigidly raising his son, had produced a man who was totally incapable of being president. When Porter died, Miles, because of his stock holdings, took over as president. He was an abject failure. After one year, the board moved him to the position of Chairman, but with no decision-making powers. Today, Miles is an unhappy, frustrated man who would be much happier working as a clerk or cashier, with limited responsibilities.

The learning of initiative, responsibility and accountability needs to start early in childhood. When children don't develop these qualities, it often turns out that these missed experiences have negative results later on. When parents fail to follow through on things like allowances, or solving school problems, they lose vital opportunities to build their children's character. By the time the parents realize that some character flaws are present, the children may be older and already out of their grasp—spending most of their time at school, playing sports and out with friends.

As Drs. Jordan and Margaret Paul put it, "Giving teenagers responsibility for their lives when they've been tightly controlled is frightening. The decisions they have to make are much more serious than those that have to be made at six or ten years old. Kids who have practice with decisions don't have so much trouble. When young children have a chance to practice making decisions, they are better equipped to make the more important decisions as they get older."[4]

Many children who inherit wealth are missing some fundamental values because they never had to work for anything while they were growing up. They weren't allowed to have a newspaper delivery route because it would interrupt the extended family vacations. They were discouraged from baby-sitting because Mom and Dad weren't available to chauffeur them around (even the chauffeur was too busy). By the time they were teenagers, they hadn't learned anything about job responsibility or how to handle money.

This is what happened with another client of ours, Hal Moreland, who had built up a 450-million-dollar business based on international, commercial real estate. Hal, himself, was the soul of integrity. He did business on his handshake, and his word was his bond. He gave value for value received, usually throwing in "a little extra" because he believed it would ultimately be more profitable than driving hard bargains. Hal personally trained all his staff to work with a creative, noncompetitive attitude. His increasing net worth confirmed that his enlightened policies worked. By the time he retired at age seventy, Hal Moreland's name had become synonymous with integrity in international real estate circles.

Unfortunately, Hal had devoted so much of his time to building the business that he had neglected his own two sons, Owen and

Cass. He had left their training to his wife, who was also absent much of the time. After she died, as they were finishing high school, the boys were left pretty much on their own. When Hal sent Owen to the Wharton School in Philadelphia, and Cass to the Harvard Business School, he told himself that he had fulfilled his parental responsibilities. Owen and Cass took over the business when Hal retired, a few years later.

I came into the picture about ten years after the sons had taken over the business. They had reduced it from a worth of 450 million to something under 150 million, and were still losing money. Their questionable tactics had nearly run the business into the ground..

Their father had built the business based on people, trust and integrity. Owen and Cass, in contrast, tried to keep it going on the basis of opportunism and tight margins. Their motto was, "Make a deal, shop around, re-deal or get out." They used slow pay to make money on the float. They interpreted the casebook lessons they had learned at Wharton and Harvard to mean, "Screw the other guy before he can screw you." Their dad, who was a model of integrity, is probably turning over in his grave because of their behavior. But it was caused, at least in part, by the fact that he had never gotten around to teaching them his values.

Teaching children self-reliance and accountability is a good way to start. Taking the training wheels off is always a judgment call, as any parent knows who is familiar with skinned knees and elbows. Money accountability helps children develop good personal values at an early age. The mistakes they make in their savings accounts, what they save money for and what they spend money on, are all small things. But as they grow up, these experiences will help them to manage bigger things and will also give an indication of their character.

Children, like adults, learn from mistakes. But it is also vitally important that lessons in self-reliance and accountability result in some measure of success for your children. If their experiences commonly result in failure, their self-esteem will be sorely damaged and they will come to view self-reliance and accountability as negatives. From my experience with clients and their families, I've come to see just how crucial a positive self-image can be. Self-image is largely built up from early childhood experiences which set in place patterns that can repeat throughout a lifetime. Even in the face of later, positive experiences, these behavior patterns tend to remain dominant and unchanging. Unfortunately, with many families, and especially families of wealth, children's negative self-images seem to be built into the family system: the dominating father has unrealistic expectations from his children and, when one of them doesn't meet his high standards, he yells something like, "What's the matter with you, dummy, can't you do anything right?" Mom typically reacts to this by trying to protect the child, but this only provides a path of temporary sanctuary for the child, it doesn't improve the child's self-image.

A few pages back, I described how a banker, Porter Scudder, had so dominated his son that the young man was totally ineffective as president of the bank. A more extreme case is that of Don Jessup, who owned a large farm equipment company. Don expected his only son, John, to grow up as he, himself had: tough and hard-hitting. When the boy failed to do this, he bore the brunt of his father's verbal abuse. Internally, he crumbled at the constant negative judgments, absorbing early and often the message that he was incompetent (and thus unlovable). Don's wife, Marilyn, in an attempt to neutralize her husband's influence on the boy, added to the tragedy by trying to raise little John gently, in accordance with what she saw as their social position. This only increased the father's abuse of his "sissy" son.

This boy never had a chance. His self-image is rooted in the belief that he is ineffective and a nonperson. His values are all oriented to avoiding pain and surviving. He has never learned how to be an independent human being and, *according to him, the greatest thing that has ever happened to him is the tremendous relief he felt when his father died.*

Many times, the busy entrepreneurial father or mother doesn't spend time with the children and tries to buy their love with money and gifts. But when the only reward or expression of love and support the children receive is money and the things that it buys, then money and possessions become the measure by which the children judge their self-worth. If, for example, a son perceives that he has received less from parents than they have given to another sibling, then that son will not only be resentful, his self-esteem will also be diminished. (The subject of treating children equally vs. fairly is covered in Chapter 16.)

Concerned parents ask the question: "How can I give my children self-esteem?" And the answer, of course, is that you can't give them self-esteem—the best you can do is to create the circumstances that may help them to develop their own self-esteem. The place to start is to avoid setting standards for your children that are based on *your* expectations. Dad, the successful entrepreneur, assumes and expects that everyone else in the world has been blessed with his initiative—including his children. Yet initiative is one thing that *cannot* be taught.

Helping build self-esteem in your children is quite similar to building self-esteem in your employees—you provide them with challenges that will stretch their abilities but not exceed them so much that you are inviting failure. Children thrive on positive reinforcement and praise (who doesn't?). Be sure to take the time to praise your children's accomplishments whenever and wherever you can. That doesn't mean that there should be no accountability—you need to let them know when they have done poorly. But it is crucial that your criticism is constructive and encouraging. Instead of the "You dummy!" style, be sure it comes out something like, "Yes, it's hard, but I know that you're smart enough (or strong enough or brave enough) to do better, and it's important that you try just as hard as you can."

Helping to build self-esteem in children is a long process that requires attention, insight and sensitivity day after day, for years. For the children of wealthy parents, there is an extra burden in the building of self-esteem. That burden is the denial of wealth. In family after family, I have found that the children think poorly of themselves, and of how others view them, because they are rich. Many of them buy their clothing in thrift stores to try to counteract their embarrassment from being rich. It's a situation where the children rarely talk about it with their parents, but are constantly aware of it.

I know young adults who have run off to less-developed countries and live in poverty, while they leave all of their money with trustees... sometimes for many years, until they get through the denial stage. One young woman wanted desperately to be treated just like her peers, but her friends found out that she went on vacations to an island off the Florida coast, and that her family owned a large part of the island. That changed something in the woman's relationships—she had suddenly become an outsider, someone different, and she hated it.

This woman now shuns any outward signs of wealth. She dresses plainly, never makes any but modest purchases and never, never talks about her family with others. She rarely gives her address or other information about where she lives to her friends. Until she felt safe enough to speak about this during one of our family meetings, this woman had never mentioned any of this to her family. She's been living a lie, pretending not to have wealth, and it's been very painful for her.

On the surface, denial of wealth is caused by not wanting to seem different from friends. But additional probing frequently reveals biases not only against accumulated wealth, but also against business and profit in general.

Ironically, the daughter of one of our clients was totally unaware that her father, a successful businessman, was one of the most beloved persons in the community, and consistently gave much of his own time and energy as well as his money for worthy causes. One conversation I had with the daughter, Diane, went like this:

"I think 'profit' is an ugly word. I don't want to have anything to do with the business."

"Wait a minute, Diane, do you think your father is an honest man?"

"Yes, I think so."

"How about integrity? Does he have integrity?"

"Yes."

"Do you think he uses money wisely? Do you know how much he does to help others?"

"Sort of, but I know he keeps a lot of it."

"Diane, have you ever heard the story of the pitcher? If you are an empty pitcher, every relationship you have is to get somebody to put something into you; but if you are a full pitcher, then you can give and give and give because you've got something to give. Have you ever thought of it that way?

"No, I guess not."

From that, the conversation went into the nature of the family business, how many people it employed, and the good that its services did. It turned out that Diane was totally ignorant of what her dad was doing—in business and in the community—she had shunned knowing because of her discomfort with wealth.

Until this young woman can start to address this issue from a healthy standpoint, she may be emotionally crippled and may never be able to be a responsible, accountable person who can inherit wealth and have it be an asset rather than a liability.

Slowly, we are trying to encourage responsible young adults not to be embarrassed by growing up with money. We have tried to help these young people to understand that money gives them options, and among these options are opportunities to do some wonderful things for humankind. They don't have to be embarrassed, they don't have to put down the family business and business in general; what they need to do is learn to be creative and help figure out the best uses for their money.

In many, many families I work with, the children dislike—even abhor—what their fathers or mothers are doing. They don't understand why they feel this way and the parents don't understand either. I've covered many of the reasons in the previous chapters: lack of communication among family members; children not understanding the business; the children seeing many of the negative influences of the business on the family, such as the time Dad spends away from home, or cash-flow crunches where the business gets all the available money while the family may have unmet needs.

Typically, Dad doesn't come roaring home and announce to the whole family that he's gotten a new contract, or that his team has just come up with a new widget and that it's tested perfectly—Dad comes home late, tired, sometimes irritated at all he's had to put up with that day. The kids see all this negative drain and stress on the family without ever seeing the positive side of what the business provides—the strokes Dad gets, and the financial reward. The subliminal message says, "Baby, if you go into business, you'd better be tough and you'd better be willing to pay a high price." They get the message and say to themselves, "This is not what I'm going to do. There has got to be an easier way to live than what my Dad goes through."

Like most problems in life, a grown-up son's or daughter's aversion to the family business often comes from ignorance. The antidote is simple. Get your kids involved. I recently spent some time with a family where I made the comment to the father that he is going to have to spend time with his daughters— spend time educating them on the nuances of how to buy and sell real estate, because that is his business. How do you go about finding a piece of property? Once you think it's a good piece of property, how do you buy it right? What are all the processes you have to go through to be able to build on it? What are the risks involved? He said to me, "Roy, that took me years and years to learn." I replied, "Isn't that exciting? Do you realize that it will take you years to teach everything to your daughters? Do you realize what a great avenue you've got for spending more time with them?" He had never looked at it that way, but he knew, instinctively, that it was true.

Some of my clients are farmers. Their sons have ridden in their pickup truck every day and have helped operate every piece of equipment from the time they were two years old. Some of those children want to be farmers as much as they want to eat or breathe. And they want to be just like Dad. In the same family, there are children who love Dad just as much but want nothing to do with the family farm. One youngster wants to be a concert pianist; another wants to be a merchant seaman. All of these dreams are okay. A passion is a passion.

How can you help your children or your grandchildren find their passion? If it is for the family business, it will probably be because you've spent a lot of time with them, and the challenge, the excitement and the rewards will have rubbed off on them, plus the realization of what a fantastic opportunity they've been given. Whatever their final choice, spend time with them on it. If your child really wants to try to become a concert pianist, take the time to check out piano teachers and schools, and go to recitals. Don't delegate it to someone else—stay involved! And remember, it's never too late.

The title of this chapter is "When the Children Are Young." That has real meaning for me because I have come to see how important early training is. When I say "early training," I'm talking about education in the broadest sense—the informal education that comes from watching Dad or Mom, or from being with another mentor. Informal education includes learning people skills: how to communicate well and to deal with people's needs and desires and complaints and idiosyncrasies. Informal education includes the ability to weigh many factors and to make sound judgment calls, based on solid values.

A deliberate mentoring program is very important. The mentor doesn't have to be Dad—it can be a friend in the same industry or in another industry. It needn't always be the same person, although the consistency and trust that comes from continuing contact is beneficial. The best mentor seems to be someone who is 20-25 years older than the youngster who is learning; someone who has been through the same experiences that the boy or girl will be going through, and who can show the way. If one of the children's mentors is a nanny, it is terribly important to choose a nanny whose values and character you respect; a nanny should be chosen with the same care you would choose a company president—and perhaps be given the same respect.

I believe that children should get acquainted, at an early age, with how business works, what real estate is all about, and why there are stock markets. Children should be able to sit in on board meetings—business boards, charitable boards—and to learn the role of a director and of the board members. As soon as possible, your children should be included in social functions where they can interact with your friends and can be exposed to diverse topics of discussion.

In primitive societies, the children learn by watching their parents interact in all kinds of situations. When the family trades camels for goats, the kids get to see how it is done, and they gradually become competent traders themselves. One of the drawbacks of our modern society is that our kids are isolated from business transactions, and they don't get to see how Dad works, and to learn from it. With your children and grandchildren, try to get them involved and let them see how you operate. After they've watched you negotiate some issue, discuss it with them and tell them, on a level they can understand, what options you had and why you made the decisions you did.

It's very important, in the formative years, to expose your children to sound values, to sound judgments, and to allow them to gain experience in the real world. As a parent, you have the opportunity to be your children's most influential teacher—don't let the early years slip away without leaving your mark.

1   Fortune Magazine, September 10, 1990

2, 3 Bronfman, Joanie, Doctoral thesis, *The Experience Of Inherited Wealth: A Social-Psychological Perspective*, UMI Dissertation Service, Ann Arbor, MI

4   Paul, Jordan and Margaret, *If You Really Loved Me*, CompCare Publishers, Minneapolis, 1987

9 Developing the Family Team

Just as your business requires a strategic plan for its continuing growth, so does the goal of preparing your children to inherit your wealth. What is a strategic plan? It can be a comprehensive plan to educate your children across a wide spectrum of life challenges, or it can have a narrower focus. The example of Willis Dryden describes a plan for teaching his grown-up children money management. Willis has a construction company worth about 70 million dollars. He has one daughter who is married, and she and her husband are both employed. Willis doesn't want his money to be a destructive influence in their lives. If they suddenly received ten million dollars, Willis was afraid that the money might be a disincentive for them to work, and that it might be disruptive to them and to his grandchildren, whom he loves dearly.

Willis and I interviewed his daughter, her husband and their children, to try to determine their attitudes toward money. Where, together, they're now making $65,000 per year, what would they do if they suddenly started receiving $25,000 more, $100,000 more or $500,000 more? These were not easy questions to answer, but we have made a start. The plan calls for Willis to form a partnership in which his daughter and son-in-law are partners in investment programs. The investment amounts range from $100,000 to $500,000. Willis owns the investments and his daughter and son-in-law receive income from them in accordance with their degree of management participation. The idea is that the youngsters won't suddenly be confronted with substantial sums; over a 20-year period, they will gradually be introduced to more money as they learn how to manage it effectively.

This kind of plan requires a commitment from Willis to spend the time educating his daughter and son-in-law. So far, he has done well, and they have increased their annual income by $25,000 and are investing it wisely.

This kind of sound, strategic planning and implementing is still relatively rare. Too often the father will say, "I don't need help with a plan—I'll do it myself." Two years later, when I inquire about how his plan is working, I typically get a reply of "What plan?"

Lack of planning for family time together is also prevalent. In many instances, Dad works himself to exhaustion and completes a big project. Then he suddenly comes home and announces, "I need to get away. We're leaving next week." This may be the only way they ever go on vacation.

Mom then has to make all kinds of changes in her calendar (including the complications· of what to do about school-age children). The sudden announcement deprives Mom of control and causes ill will between the couple. It's hard for the wife to coerce her husband into doing vacation planning because she doesn't know the cash flow situation of the business and how much money is available for trips. Nor does she know when her husband's work load will allow him to take time off. From his side, Dad resists vacation planning because he is so bound up in his business priorities. *And while he is quite capable of planning business conferences and major capital purchases a year in advance, he cannot seem to give family activities the same high priority—they occur "when there is time."*

One of the recommendations I make to my clients' families is that they set up a family calendar and create a family fun fund. In Chapter 6, I described how the children of Hugh and Emy McDowell planned an entire vacation by themselves, and how successful it was. Based on that experience, Hugh initially set up a $200,000 fun fund. From various business opportunities he had, he gradually built it up to $5,000,000. Each year, the fund generates about $400,000 in income. It is separate from the business, so Hugh doesn't have to worry about money being taken from the business.

Each November, the family members plan their fun calendar for the next year. Hugh can structure his time away from the business because he knows, well in advance, the dates to which he is committed.

Emy knows how much income the fund will generate each year and she is in charge of the fun budget. Like Hugh, she can now schedule her own time and commitments, and she can make convenient arrangements for the children to take time off.

Hugh, Emy and the children decide, together, what constitutes "fun." While the fun fund was at first used exclusively for going on family trips together, as the children have matured and the amount in the fund has increased, "fun" now includes hands-on involvement with charitable causes.

The family time together has been a wonderful experience for the McDowells. For the first time since his wife and children can remember, Dad is putting aside time just to be with them. Hugh's wife, Emy, is delighted with the new arrangement. The planned, regular vacations have kept Hugh healthier and more vigorous. And Emy feels that she has more control in family affairs and a real voice in decision-making. The whole family is operating more as a team.

What happens with the many clients who have established family fun funds is that Dad has started to take family activities as seriously as he does the business. Family fun activities are planned the way any business activity is planned so that, in November, Dad knows what his commitments are for the following year. Family activities no longer get"bumped" from the calendar by business or other personal affairs. So far, with the aid of this system, none of my clients have gone back on their family commitments.

The idea for a family calendar started years ago when I realized I needed to spend more time with my own family. I got together at home with my wife, Diana, and our children, and showed them my year-at-a-glance business calendar. At that time I was doing a lot of public speaking around the country, and some of my lecture commitments were a year or more in advance. Each November, I blocked out my time commitments on that calendar. So I said, "Here are my current commitments. What dates do you want?"

I have three sons, and their schedules were complicated by the fact that each one went to a different school. Eric told me he wanted me to come to his football games. Danny and Scott wanted me to come to their basketball games. So we had to figure out how to plan my time with the boys, and our vacations and other family activities, and still accommodate all of my business commitments. I also told the boys that if I committed myself to time with them, it was necessary that I spend some time away from home, earning money, and I wanted their full support in this.

We made up a year-long family calendar that year and each subsequent year that the boys were living at home. After that commitment, I don't think I ever missed a football or basketball game, and we all had marvelous times together. I didn't make as much money as I might otherwise have, but my relationship with each of my sons is very, very good.

If you don't include family activities in your schedule and you are deeply involved in running your business, it's very difficult to find enough time for family activities. Even when you do manage it, you are squeezing either the business or your family and it is a stressful situation. Creating a family activities calendar provides a useful structure to elevate and maintain family priorities. It has become one of the standard tools I recommend for all of my clients.

While part of the task of developing a family team is to raise the priority level of activities you share with your children, part of the task is learning to allow the children more independence at the same time. One day my youngest son, Danny, telephoned me from college. "Dad, I'm broke. I need some money." "That's wonderful," I told him. "What do you mean, 'That's wonderful?'" he replied, obviously puzzled. "Because you're going to learn what it means to be broke," I said. "Isn't that exciting?" "But Dad," Danny said, "I only need $200." I remained firm. "It doesn't make any difference if it's $200 or $200,000. It's the same thing that you need to learn. I know you'll come up with the money somehow, or decide that you really don't need it all that badly. In the process, you'll learn how to avoid going broke again."

It was a hard thing for me to do. It's easy to love with money...to just give it to them...but it's a lot harder to love by denying them and risking their feelings for you. In this case, it turned out to be worth it. Three years later, when my son and I were talking together, he said, "When you wouldn't send me that $200, I hated you, just hated you." I asked him what he had done about the money at that time. "Well, I had spent my monthly allotment on junk and then I discovered I needed to buy some books for a lab. So I went to the student loan office and got a loan and paid it off over the next three months. I guess you were right about my learning, because I haven't been broke since then."

Danny had found his own way out of his troubles, growing in the process. With Danny, my instinct had proved correct. But deciding whether to give in to your children's needs or refuse them in hope of teaching them a lesson is sometimes a difficult judgment call. In the case of Josh Park, a client of mine in New England, his son and daughter-in-law and their two small children were in trouble. They had just barely made their latest mortgage payment, and they were out of food. Josh and his wife invited them all over for dinner to discuss the problem. Here is Josh's version of what happened.

"We went over their present finances, how they got there, and what they could do about it. We didn't rescue them with money, though it would have been so easy. Instead, we restrained ourselves and talked with them about how they could raise some short-term cash. My son, Joel, was in real estate and he had two deals going that wouldn't close for another sixty days. I advised him that he might get a bank loan based on his accounts receivable, if his boss verified that the deals were sound. Also, he could refinance their house or sell one of their three cars.

"As it turned out, the bank wouldn't loan them any money. Joel did manage to close one of his real estate deals, and that gave them enough to exist for a few weeks. Then they sold one car, whittled down the utility bills, and cut nonessentials. This was a totally new experience for them—they'd never had to tighten their belts like that before. I thought they had done a good job at getting in the black.

"I'd been through many, many belt-tightening experiences, myself, and it was not a big deal for me. But I guess I misread how strongly the situation had affected them because a month later we discovered that Joel had a bleeding ulcer. That's when I felt that I had made a wrong decision. Loving your son by teaching him a lesson is one thing—hurting him is another. I did a lot of soul-searching after that, trying to figure out if my principles were really valid or if I was trying to remake Joel in my own image.

"Two or three months later, Joel's wife, Nicole, confided to me that it had been a very difficult situation for them, but that the crisis really drew them together as a family. Joel's ulcer faded after a few more months, and all their bills got paid up—by them. I feel that I did the right thing, but I still have some guilt about it."

It's tough. Young people need to have their training wheels removed so they can try balancing on their own. They need to face mistakes and failure, and to know what it's like to pick themselves up and push on again. They need to build their own strong, self-confident images, preferably laced with a little humility. And they need to learn to be responsible and accountable—to themselves and to others.

When your children are in need, whether or not you decide to financially assist them is not the most important element in dealing with the issue; the most important element is how much you are personally involved. When you take a personal interest in their problems (if invited to do so), it shows them you care. Nothing else—nothing—can take the place of your personal involvement.

One of the mistakes successful entrepreneurs may make as parents is to treat their children with kid gloves, sparing them the rigors of responsibility and accountability. The case of Norm Schroeder illustrates my point. Norm grew up in extreme hardship, where his family was hard-pressed to feed all the children. Norm was self-taught all the way, and it was a hard climb to success. Today, he is a manufacturer of turbine components in Portland, Oregon, and his international sales are over 50 million. Norm's son, Jack, came to work for him a few years ago and Norm bent over backwards to give his son every opportunity that he, himself, had been denied. Unfortunately, that included treating him differently from the other employees. Jack soon learned that, as the boss's son, he could get away with just about anything.

When Norm hired a new Production Manager, Jack quickly let it be known that his privileged position meant that he wasn't to be ordered around. The manager knew that he had to run the plant or leave it. Without hesitating, he faced Jack and told him, "If you don't do what I've told you to do within the next 30 minutes, you're no longer going to be employed here." He then immediately reported the incident to Norm.

Norm backed the manager one hundred per cent. He called his son in and did something he should have done years earlier. He said: "I hired the new manager to do a job and his job is to run the plant. If you ever challenge his authority again, I have told him he can fire you on the spot. As for you, I'm sorry that I haven't said this before now, but maybe it's not too late. From now on you're on your own here. No more hanging on my shirttails and acting like the boss's son. I happen to think you're smart enough and competent enough to make it on your own. If you don't agree and if you don't think you're good enough to compete on that basis, you should leave."

This was a real shock to Jack—he'd never heard anything like that before. To give him credit, he stopped testing to see how much he could get away with and he started acting like a member of the team. It was a real turning point in his life. That was six years ago. He's now Vice President for Research and he's doing a great job—he's helped the company successfully obtain dozens of new patents that are proving to be very lucrative.

After teaching children responsibility and accountability, one of the next steps is allowing them to test their values and to take risks. Ironically, although entrepreneurs have had to become expert risk-takers themselves, they often fail to teach their children these skills. As parents (and grandparents), this is difficult to do because it goes against their protective instincts. But like it or not, children are constantly exposed to risks—in school, in sports, relationships. And often their failures do more for them than their successes.

Sometimes, youngsters take risks that are inherently unwise, and they need to learn how to assess risks before they undertake something. When they have taken a reasonable risk and have failed, it's important to help them examine the effort that went into it. For example, what else could they have done? What did they miss? Was it mental or physical effort that was lacking, or was it a deficiency in spirit? Are they willing to put more effort into it the next time? In other words, are they willing to overcome obstacles in order to gain rewards?

Value-testing and risk-taking are necessary maturing processes—when young adults don't have opportunities to test the values they have received from their parents and to take risks and assess the results, their development suffers. In Chapter 2, I mentioned the case of Tom Wilbanks, who gave his daughter, Lynn, $10,000 to invest "as she pleased," but filled the air with dire pronouncements about the instability of the stock market, the hidden pitfalls in real estate, etc. Lynn placed the $10,000 in CD's and was never able to accept any degree of risk. All her adolescent years, her father had been giving her a mixed message: take risks but don't take risks. She chose the latter.

Children have to fail in order to learn what success means. They have to lie and suffer the consequences in order to really appreciate integrity. And they have to learn to rely on others and become part of a team in order to accomplish a goal.

These points are illustrated in a classic story by Mark Twain called, *The Man Who Corrupted Hadleyburg*. In the story, the town of Hadleyburg has the reputation of having the highest morals in the country—and all the residents of Hadleyburg agree. One day a stranger comes to town with a sack of gold, and leaves instructions that it be given to an individual in town who had done a certain good deed in the past. The fun comes from the fact that the good deed never happened, and everyone in town scrambles for the gold by claiming to be the one who had done it.

Twain's point is that we don't really know morality until we've been sorely tempted in the opposite direction. Similarly, with our children and grandchildren, we can't just teach them—we have to let them experience life for themselves. Some children grow up and spend their entire adults lives with their training wheels still on. This is compounded by the naturally-increasing conservatism of the mature entrepreneur. As entrepreneurs get older, they'll start to hedge their bets. The older they get, the more they want to put aside. The conflict comes about when the mature entrepreneur has an entrepreneurial, grown-up son or daughter who is ready to take some risks. But Dad says, "You risk your money—I'm not risking mine anymore." Then Dad has to find a way to teach the principles of reasonable risk-taking, using either his child's money or with a limited sum of his own. It's an unfortunate irony when Dad, who made his fortune by thoughtful risk-taking, is unable to help his own children to do the same.

Whether you decide to financially assist your children or not, the most important element in dealing with them is not how much money you give them, it's how much you are personally involved. *Nothing can take the place of you demonstrating you care by taking a personal interest in their lives.*

10 The Use of Money

John Kolski had seen money destroy too many families, and he felt strongly that he didn't want it to be a destructive influence in the lives of his own children. When they were teenagers, he informed his son and daughter that his entire estate, aside from the expense of their college education, would be going to charity—they would receive nothing. During college, they worked at part-time jobs to have some extra spending money. After graduating, both the son and the daughter found jobs and were responsible for themselves, never receiving a penny from Dad or Mom. They were making modest salaries, earning their own way.

When I became involved as facilitator for John's family, one of the things we discussed was the use of money. I used the analogy of a tape recorder and asked whether the electricity that powers the recorder is good or bad. Everyone understood, of course, that the electricity is a neutral force for tape recording. If I record lies in order to harm someone, then I am using that force negatively. But if I record an inspiring or informative selection that really helps someone, then I am using the force positively. Similarly, money is a neutral force that can be used either for bad or good.

In family board meetings, John, his wife and children and I continued to discuss the idea of money as a neutral, but potentially positive tool. After some time, John came to realize that giving money or not giving money to his children wasn't the issue—helping or harming his children was the issue. And with the tools the family was beginning to use—value clarification, the family advisory board, starting family partnerships, investment education and so on, John saw that his son and his daughter were developing enough maturity that he could trust their ability to handle money.

John changed his will and trust documents to reflect his new confidence toward his children. And since he has done so, an interesting change has come about in both the daughter and the son. With substantial assets now under their control, they are beginning to act with considerable confidence and responsibility toward *everything* they deal with. I believe it is at least partly because they know their dad is now saying, "I trust you with money."

Where his son and daughter were each earning only $20,000 a year, in addition they are now sharing the income from a million dollars—about $100,000 a year. They have continued working in their jobs and are reinvesting that new income wisely. And Dad, in turn, has seen that money can be a positive influence in the life of young adults.

John Kolski is typical of many of my clients in that he is very balanced with money matters. John knows how to save and he also knows how to spend for good purposes. With others, that isn't always the case. The lack of balanced judgment often shows up in small matters. For example, after a board meeting with a family in Indianapolis, the youngsters wanted to go out to the nearby fast-food restaurant for a snack. I couldn't believe what the father said then: "Let's drink our drinks here, we've got lots of soft drinks here." "Why?" I asked, "Don't you like drinks with your hamburgers?" "Yes," he said, "but they make all their profits on the drinks." This was from a man worth at least 30 million. The message he was sending to his children was that no one was entitled to make profits except him.

When stinginess has to do with petty things, it's merely annoying to be around. But when real human needs are at stake, monetary mean-spiritedness is more tragic. I worked with one particular client (ex-client now) for several years—I'll call him George. During the last year I worked with him, in addition to counseling his family, I was able to pass on some ideas to George that enabled him to make an extra half million dollars. He was already quite a wealthy man, probably worth something over twenty million.

That summer, I volunteered to do some fund-raising for a very effective local camp for under-privileged boys and girls. I had committed to raising money to send six children to camp for the summer—at $1500 per child. I had put in my own $1500 and I wanted to find five others to pledge the amount for one youngster each. When I put it to George, he asked: "Who's doing this?" I told him the names of the people involved and how effective the camp had been in helping poor kids get a valuable experience. Then George asked, "How much profit do they make on each kid?" I said, "I don't know. Who cares? They're doing a great job for these kids. I've seen these kids after camp, and it's really something positive." Although George had spent many years aggressively pursuing profits himself, he declined to participate because he was afraid someone else might be making a profit.

These examples notwithstanding, in my experience most possessors of wealth are not interested in money for itself and they are balanced and reasonable in its use. In fact, of all my clients, not a single one is obsessed with money. What they *are* obsessed with is accepting challenges and solving problems in order to make something work, to create something of value. It's the challenge that inspires them, not the love of money.

In our society, children are not taught a philosophy of money. As parents, we need to make a conscious effort to teach our children that money is not good or bad by itself—it's something that will give them options. With money, they can have a choice of what to eat or drink, while impoverished people must take anything they can get. With money, children have the option of working, enrolling in an inexpensive junior college or going to a top-ranked university—lacking money, their choices are more limited.

Our children need to understand that having money does not make someone a good or a bad person. There are good people who are rich and there are bad people who are rich, just as there are good and bad people who are poor. And as we teach our children how money creates more wealth and productivity and jobs through the family business, we also need to teach them that the use of money can also be other-directed. One way to do this is to include some philanthropic element in trusts. Because the trust involves them in some kind of charitable endeavor, it makes children aware of the importance of philanthropy in their lives. The philanthropic element also helps to assuage guilt they may be carrying when they inherit sizeable wealth, and it justifies their inheritance. Some of the grown-up children of my clients have gone a long way toward solving their problems with wealth by adopting an *active* philanthropic focus, giving not only their money, but their time and energy as well.

Money can be used in ways that give it a life of its own so that its benefits multiply throughout society. Anita Roddick is one of the contemporary role models I like to use to illustrate how a business and its profits can be used in socially responsible ways. Anita is founder of the British-based cosmetics company called The Body Shop, which had burgeoning sales of over 140 million at the end of its 1990 fiscal year. The Body Shop operates in 37 countries now, and analysts predict that it will sustain a growth rate of 40-50% per year for many years. The company is as well known for its social causes as for its products and has become one of the emerging symbols of a new business consciousness.

Anita raises the most fundamental questions about business: what do customers really want from a product, and what do employees really want from their work? Customers, she claims, are intelligent people who want genuine, factual and useful information about products, not more advertising hype. And so each Body Shop retail store is filled with everything from note cards to pamphlets to reference manuals to video presentations, giving the customer as much information about the products as he or she would like. These information sources tell where the raw materials come from, how they are tested (no animal testing), how they are refined and blended, and the results when they are used. There are no photographs of semi-nude models, no fantasies of instant rejuvenation or romantic appeal—just straight, useful information and quality products.

Amazingly, the company *does no advertising*, but relies on establishing credibility with customers by educating them, and obtains new customers by word-of-mouth. The effect on customers is that the company is playing straight with them—it isn't trying to trick them into buying anything.

Anita insists that all employees be treated the same way as customers. She believes that employees, in general, are cynical about the companies they work for because they understand that they are viewed by management as mere tools for making profits. They come to work because they need the money, and they do what is minimally required of them to keep their job. In general, employees are simply not interested in how much profit the company makes, nor is there much reason to be. In contrast, The Body Shop devotes a great deal of time to educating its employees. This training is not about selling or on how to maximize profits, but covers the nature of the products and their uses. *The training is as much designed to educate and uplift the employee as it is to help the customer.* While most companies have to drag their employees to training programs that the employee is not really interested in, The Body Shop schools are constantly filled and there is a waiting list to attend. All training is free.

In addition to humanizing customers and employees, the company is very active in a wide range of social causes. It mobilizes employees for petition drives for humanitarian causes, and it donates substantial sums for environmental concerns such as saving whales and preserving rain forests. It instructs and aids villagers in undeveloped countries in preparing local materials so that they can become suppliers for the company. And it has built a factory in an impoverished urban area for the specific purpose of hiring people who are traditionally unemployable. Each retail store is required to have a community project, and the company pays each store employee to spend some time each week on that project.

Anita is not just successfully selling cosmetics. She is empowering people by encouraging and aiding their natural passion for helping others. The bonds between management, employees and customers that have brought such success to The Body Shop are based on the belief that the purpose of business, by virtue of its talent, energy and resources, is *direct involvement* in solving major social problems. Anita's vision is to totally rewrite the book on business. Utopian fantasy? So far, her company is living up to her vision.

While many corporations, and families of wealth, contribute generously to charitable organizations, there is often very little involvement or follow-up to determine whether or not the money is being used effectively. Part of my role as family facilitator is to get clients' family members—particularly grown-up children—involved with philanthropy. It's important that family members have a real feeling for the causes they want to help. The first thing we do together is to use Abraham Maslow's "Hierarchy Of Needs"[1] as a guide.

This helps family members decide if they feel closer to organizations which provide food and shelter, tackle environmental problems or support the arts, etc. When we have identified the causes that family members feel strongly about, I ask them to research the organizations that address those needs.

A part of this research involves finding out how efficient a particular charitable organization is—that is, what percentage of its income actually goes toward its stated purpose and what percentage is used for administrative costs and fund-raising. Some organizations actually spend a majority of their income on fund-raising. This is usually a real eye-opener, especially to the sons and daughters. Each charitable organization has this information available to potential donors. It is also available for most major charities from certain periodicals and private organizations.[2]

I ask the sons and daughters to personally check out the organizations of their choice to see if they like working with the staff members, and to get as much first-hand information as they can about the work the organization is accomplishing. When family members have decided, together, what organizations they want to support, I next introduce a time/money guideline. Dad and Mom, and any advisers that are needed, determine how much money will be available for charitable causes. Then I ask the sons and daughters what amount of total time they are willing to devote to charitable causes and, of that total time, how much time they are willing to give to each organization. The guideline requires that they can only give money to an organization in proportion to the amount of time they are willing to work with that organization. For example, assume that $100,000 is available for donations, and all sons and daughters, together, commit themselves to giving twenty hours of their time per month. Then, if they want to give half of that money to a particular charity, they must spend at least half of their time, or 10 hours, working directly with that charity.

This forces them to know what is going on with the charity of their choice, and how their money is being used. Parents love this system because it imposes discipline and responsibility on their children and because the involvement is a real education for them.

I have a client and close friend, Bob Graham, (I'm using his real name with his permission) who is an exemplary role model for the good use of money. In his travels in the 1970's, Bob developed an acute awareness of the disparity and resources between the U.S. and the Third World. Vowing to do what he could to help, Bob decided he would implement a "50/50 at 50" plan. When he turned fifty years old, he would devote half his time and resources to service.

In 1985, Bob founded a non-profit international development organization called Katalysis. Working closely with indigenous, self-help groups in Belize, Honduras and the Caribbean, Katalysis has helped thousands of poor farmers and small business owners, disadvantaged women and unemployed youths gain the skills and resources to become self-reliant.

Bob, his wife, and his six children are all active in philanthropic work. The family meets twice a year to review their "social investments." In addition to teaching his children about *using* money, Bob also engages his children in projects that *make* money. The family's joint involvement with philanthropy and money management has been a challenging process that has taken considerable time and effort to work out, but it has brought the family much closer together.

Bob Graham is a man who knows that money can be used for much more than just making more money. Through his socially-responsible projects, he has not only helped countless others but has enriched his own life and the lives of his children as well.

While wealth does confer responsibility, it also provides unique opportunities. Some wonderful things can happen through the creative use of wealth: profound benefits for society, and immense education, satisfaction and fulfillment to the families who have learned to work together to make it happen.

1   Maslow, Abraham, "A Theory of Human Motivation,"
    <u>Psychological Review</u>, Volume 50 (1943). Maslow describes
    human needs as a pyramidal hierarchy, where each need
    cannot be met until the need below it is first met.

2   An extensive listing of charities is in Consumer's Digest,
    March-April, 1989, "Where Does Your Money Go?"

    The Better Business Bureau publishes a listing of national
    charities through its Philanthropic Advisory Service, 4200
    Wilson Blvd, Arlington, VA 22203.

    The "Wise Giving Guide" is available from the National
    Charities Information Bureau, Inc, 19 Union Square West, 6th
    Floor, New York, NY 10003.

    A listing of evangelical charities is available from The
    Evangelical Council For Financial Accountability, P.O. Box
    17456, Washington, DC 20041.

11 Involving Your Family With Money

The ability to manage money isn't inherited, it is a skill which has to be learned. John D. Rockefeller Jr. certainly believed that, for he raised his children in an atmosphere of stern monetary discipline, even though they were surrounded by servants and luxury. Each child had to keep an account book of his weekly allowance, extra earnings and expenditures. The allowances were so low that the children had to do extra work around the house in order to have any pocket money. In our own families, we may not elect to have such strict discipline with our children, but we certainly should not leave the development of their money skills to chance.

With young children, school vacations are good times to give them experience in handling money when they are less busy with homework and school-related activities. One idea that works well is to let them pay all household bills during a summer. This allows the children to learn the value of electricity and water supplies, the costs of automobile, food, clothing, medical and other purchases. At an early age (perhaps 13-14, depending on maturity), I suggest you arrange for your children to get checking accounts and credit cards, with limits on them. I usually recommend beginning with $25 limits. Together with this privilege is the requirement that each week, or month, they must show you a balanced checkbook and a fully-paid-up credit card. I also suggest that you offer to match any amounts your children earn, from allowances and extra jobs, that they are able to save. Children have to learn how to make money, how to keep it, how to spend it and how to deal with debt. The checking account, credit card and the ability to earn more by saving (from your matching funds), empower your children, and though they will make mistakes, they'll learn from them and will become more responsible and accountable. Also, this kind of parent-child cooperation will help you to enhance good family communication on a topic with which you are at ease and well versed.

From the time your children are small to when they become young adults, the more time you can spend with them sharing your business and financial knowledge, the more prepared they will be to handle wealth. After they have completed college and are working and/or parenting, even if they have received an MBA, I recommend that you send each of your children to one of the small business programs available at several universities or at OMBI.₁ They teach a broad range of practical business issues which aren't found in academic programs. These small business courses aren't cheap, but they will educate your children to the point where you and they can talk the same language when it comes to the family business and finances.

In families of affluence, one of the things that taints the possession of wealth for the children is the secrecy with which the subject is surrounded. Many children grow up with the feeling that the family money must be bad because its specific value must be hidden and never discussed openly. In addition, the children get the message that they cannot be trusted with this information. By avoiding the subject, the childhood attitude that something is wrong about having money may persist into adulthood. Of course, for the grownup children, there are also societal pressures of not wanting to seem ostentatious, and fearing that if friends know they are wealthy, the friendship will be threatened. But the negative, early childhood feelings about money seem to persist in many cases.

Here are a few comments from grownup children of wealthy parents, about hiding their wealth:

> "If my roommates or somebody went out and bought a dress or some shoes and boots, they would come home and parade it. I would bring it home in a brown bag and run it up to my room and hope nobody had seen it, and hide it, and then a few days later when I would wear it and somebody would comment on it, I would say, 'Oh no, I've had this for years.' "

"I was trying very hard to hide and it meant that I couldn't talk about anything related to my background. After a while...I felt that there was nothing I could share, that there was nothing it was okay to talk about."

"I was always terrified they were going to find out somehow, and very often they did. I think I came across as being a very retentive, unsharing person who kept much, a whole lot, to himself."₂

In early family discussions having to do with family wealth, Mom and Dad usually talk in generalities. They'll ask me to present general information to the family on the subjects of estate taxes, charitable gifts, and so on, but not about specific numbers. There is a valid reason for this. When a child is five years old and asks, "Where did I come from?" there are a variety of possible answers. In one case, the mother gave a detailed reply about the human reproductive system. When she had finished, the little boy commented, "Mom, I didn't want to know all that, I just wanted to know if we're from Cincinnati like my friend Tommy."

The young child isn't prepared to understand all the details. It's a similar situation with specific questions about money: children, even grownup children, have to be prepared for dealing with specific figures. Even though family finances are discussed in generalities, it is important that the subject be treated openly because *young children already know when their family is wealthy.* This comes from simple impressions, like the fact that their home is bigger than those of their friends, it has more telephones and other appliances, and so on. Denying wealth simply creates mistrust of parents.

If the topic of specific numbers is off limits, it is important to state this openly to the children—that this subject is not going to be discussed for a while. It is a legitimate position and, because it is treated openly and directly, the children will probably accept that. They know they are not ready. The problems occur when, instead of simply stating their position, the parents hedge and waffle on the subject. Then the children feel their parents are hiding something, with all the ensuing attitudes that are picked up and carried to adulthood.

As the children grow up and become more knowledgeable about money management, *and are mature enough to handle it*, Dad and Mom should divulge more information on a step-by-step basis. Parents have a tendency to withhold this information even after the children are ready for it. At the same time, this is a highly personal decision for the parents—they have to feel comfortable talking about specific numbers with their children. To clarify the decision, it's sometimes helpful to raise this question: What good will it do, and what possible harm will it do to for the children to know the details of family wealth?

With my clients, I have found that one of the best ways to begin to involve children with family assets is to set up informal family investment partnerships. These can start when the children are in their high school or college years, or when they have left home and are married. Whatever age the children are, the dollar numbers have to be large enough to get their attention. As an example, let's look at the partnership I helped set up for Leonard and Gail Hansen and their two sons and two daughters, ages 19 to 28.

In this case, the initial funding was $500,000. If the partnership investments yield a 10% return, $50,000 will be earned the first year; if the yield is 15%, the income will be $75,000. That makes the sons and daughters sit up and pay attention. This is no longer some abstract discussion about succession, which will impact them twenty-five years later—it is real income that is happening now.

The Hansens decided to initially share the income from the partnership on a basis of 70% to Dad and Mom and 30% to be divided among their children. While Leonard and his wife, Gail, provide the capital, the sons and daughters actively participate by helping to evaluate and select a money manager, and by monitoring his performance. As the young men and women learn more about investing, and their participation becomes more valuable, the percentage of income they receive will increase.

The income that the sons and daughters earn from this partnership is theirs to do with as they wish. Will they consume it or reinvest it? How they handle this income gives Dad a good opportunity to judge their current attitudes about money. Another of Leonard's objectives for the partnership is to have good family communication about investing. Some of the questions the Hansens now discuss are: What are we going to invest in this year? What level of risk are we willing to accept? Do we need outside experts to evaluate the kinds of investments we are interested in selecting? This is a great way to get their grown-up children involved and educated and to learn to work as a team. Though the rewards begin the first year, I encourage both parents and their children to view the investment partnership as a long-term effort, stretching ahead for fifteen to twenty years. The long-term goal for the Hansen family is that by working together each year, even though their children marry and create their own families, all of the family members will gradually begin to think of themselves as a coordinated team where all participants benefit.

In my own family, I formed a different kind of partnership with my three sons. One of my main goals was for my wife and my sons to learn about partnerships. In this partnership, my wife and I were 1% owners and general partners, and my sons (and myself also) were limited partners. As general partners, my wife and I controlled the assets, but the partnership agreement gave the first 10% of all income to the limited partners. So my sons had a strong interest in making the partnership profitable.

This partnership owned a building, and we had to decide who was going to manage it. As it turned out, my wife became manager and, since she didn't have any background in managing buildings, there was much for her to learn. Our sons had to confer regularly with her in order to make the operation work, so it was also a good way to stimulate communication.

While partnerships which include all family members are very helpful in promoting family teamwork, separate partnerships between dad (or mom) and each sibling are also useful. For example, if one of your daughters becomes interested in buying a building, parent and daughter can establish a separate partnership devoted to that purpose without having to involve the whole family. This allows the young woman room to learn and take risks on her own. Sometimes there are legal requirements which limit the activities of an existing partnership, so that if new activities are to be pursued, new partnerships have to be established. Separate partnerships between parents and their children also teach how unrelated partners can work together where, for example, one partner has the capital but no time or interest in active participation, and the other partner has no capital but has energy and motivation to get things done. This type of partnership also permits a close, one-on-one relationship between Dad or Mom and each sibling.

Legal partnerships, between a parent and one son or daughter, can also include a buy/sell agreement which indicates how either partner can dissolve the partnership and get out. This provides the basis for determining each partner's capital and/or energy contribution, and how much each partner will receive from partnership assets.

While legal partnerships between parents and their children are good teaching tools, they require a strong commitment from parents because of the necessary paperwork, including filing partnership tax returns. They also require that Dad, who has probably functioned as an independent decision-maker in the past, now has to coordinate with his sons and daughters to make partnership decisions. This became a critical issue with one of my clients, Elmo Budd, and his two sons, in their late 20's. Elmo wanted to involve his sons in a partnership venture, a start-up brewery that looked like a good deal. He said he was going to commit $500,000 to it. Though the sons were both college graduates, they had had no experience with partnerships, and they waited for some word from their father about what to do next. They waited for several months and finally asked their mother, who was more approachable, what had happened to the brewery deal. Mom told them that Dad had decided it wasn't a good deal after all, and had dropped the plan.

True to his old habits, Dad hadn't discussed anything with them even though they were supposed to be partners. At a family meeting, this subject was raised and the sons said to me, "We don't want to be partners with Dad because being partners means we have nothing to say and no voice in the decisions." I then discussed with them how a real partner can't move without the consent of the other partners, and they responded with, "Well, our partner didn't act in good faith." This was terribly embarrassing for Elmo, who was seated not ten feet away. He knew they were right and he felt badly he hadn't followed through on consulting with his sons.

Many good things came out of this. His sons not only learned what a partnership was supposed to be, they learned that they could challenge a partner, even if it was their father. For his part, Elmo learned the importance of keeping an agreement with his sons. This is a particularly crucial point! I cannot emphasize enough the importance of parents keeping their promises to their children. There was another important thing Elmo had to learn from this experience. He was forced to move out of an entrepreneurial role, out of the father role, to a peer level where he was a team player.

Elmo did finally explain to his sons why the brewery was a bad investment and their communication began to improve. Ultimately, they found better investments and their subsequent partnerships have been successful.

The effects of a partnership on family relationships and on the children are impressive. When the partnership is working as it should, it is a powerful educational tool. Imagine the confidence that comes when one or more of the sons and daughters, together with Dad, have bought a piece of property, created a joint venture, or learned about managing a building or a shopping center. Imagine the effect when a son or daughter can say, "I earned $20,000 and paid my own taxes on it. Now I can pay for my own education—Dad doesn't have to give me the money." What a sense of pride and accomplishment and independence! And Dad is no longer viewed as a hard-nosed businessman who doles out pittances; now he's a trusted partner.

When families have the resources of a million or more dollars available, I recommend the creation of a Family Bank. The purpose of the Family Bank is to encourage, analyze and fund business investment ideas from any of the children. All family members are Directors of the Family Bank's Board, and loans can only be made when all Directors unanimously agree to fund an investment.

For example, a daughter may approach Dad with an investment idea.

"I think there's real opportunity in growing orchids, Dad."

"Fine," says Dad, "present a business plan to the Board."

"What's a business plan, Dad?"

"I could tell you, but it would be better for you to find a good book on the subject or go to a business professor at the local university and find out for yourself. Then you can put it together and present it."

"Will the Board approve it if I do that?"

"I can't answer for the Board," Dad says. "Just as a bank evaluates a business plan before granting a loan, the Family Bank Board will evaluate your plan and they may or may not approve funding."

With Dad's help, augmented by an outside adviser as needed, the other family members act as loan officers of the Family Bank. They evaluate the character and experience of the applicant, the risks involved, any collateral that is in place, profit potential, soundness of the plan's projections, overall chances for success, and so on. What an extraordinary education this is for the family. By doing this, family members are learning the whole process of banking, business plans, loans and paybacks. The family is growing from the experience and, if the Family Bank approves the investment loan, the interest on it will be paid to the family instead of to a commercial bank (If the Family Bank disapproves the loan, the children can still apply for a loan from a commercial bank because they have done their homework). It is an effective way to encourage and teach children to become more self-sufficient, and it is an equally good way to teach family members to be effective custodians of their wealth.

While Dad, as family entrepreneur, has had a lot of experience managing a business, he probably is not nearly as experienced in managing passive income—that is, income which comes from assets outside the business over which he has no management control. One client of mine, Gregg Pergem, sold his company and ended up with eighty million dollars after taxes. Because he didn't know what else to do with the money, he put much of it in CD's, at one hundred thousand dollars each. He had banks calling him every day, and he had stacks of bank messages on his desk, asking, "Should we roll this over? What are your instructions?" He was very frustrated. This man was a Stanford Business School graduate and a very sharp businessman, but he simply had no experience handling passive income.

One of the things which all of our facilitators at The Williams Group do is help a family plan, together, how to manage their wealth. When we meet, we usually find out that no family members want to spend the next ten years learning all there is to know about becoming, for example, a securities analyst. But questions arise such as whether or not it makes sense to invest in equity markets or debt instruments. It quickly becomes apparent that the family may need the help of a professional money manager.

Before the family hires a money manager, we ask them to agree on some subjective investment criteria. For example, are they opposed to South African investments? Are they opposed to defense contractors who are engaged in designing weapons of mass destruction? Do they favor certain investments such as companies breaking new ground in conservation, medicine or education?

When the investing criteria are in place, we ask the family to agree on risk limits. For example, if you gave a money manager one million dollars and one year later he told you it is worth only three hundred thousand, would you fire him? The odds are pretty high that you would. How about if that same money manager told you, at year's end, that your one million had yielded a return that was only one half of what you would have received from a bank or treasury note? Certainly you'd find out why the return was low, but would you fire him? How much are you willing to lose before you fire him?

Convenience is also an important part of the family's relationship with a money manager. Will the family members want to talk frequently with the money manager? Will they need to see him in person? Does the family want the money manager to be on Wall Street or is Los Angeles okay? As we start to get the various criteria together for a money manager, we run the information through our affiliates who maintain a file of several thousand money managers in the U.S. If the family wants a return of two percentage points above the prime rate, we'll determine which managers have consistently performed this well over the last ten years.

Additional criteria continue to narrow the choices. What are the minimum amounts a money manager will handle? Some won't accept you unless you have ten million or more to invest. We recommend to our clients that they begin with a $500,000 or more parent-to-child investment partnership. We tell prospective money managers that this is just the initial amount—that more is available to invest—and most will accept that. Out of the thousands of money managers, the family's criteria and the money manager's own criteria have now culled the list down to less than a dozen prospects. Next, we send out letters to each of them, asking, "Will you accept these clients under these specified conditions?" Often, we will end up with four or five money managers who will respond affirmatively. Then we arrange for these individuals to come for interviews with the family.

Alternately, we may recommend that our clients select a "manager of managers." This person chooses money managers for the family and coordinates the program for the family.

The young adults participate in all phases of this, and the family selects the ones with whom they want to work. We provide a checklist for each family member which helps them remember the positions and opinions of each money manager they have interviewed. At the end of the interviews, which may take one or two days, the family members then review all of the criteria and personal impressions, and they select their money managers.

The process doesn't end with the selection of money managers. On behalf of the family, we will closely monitor the money managers on a monthly basis. This not only includes their performance: we also watch their firms to see if any principals have left the firm or if other major changes have occurred. For example, a money manager that our clients's family selected may have had a $500,000 investment minimum but has since raised that to $2,000,000. If this is the case, he may have handed the portfolio to a junior partner who is not as experienced. This is important because our client's family has chosen *individuals* to manage their money, not companies. If there are changes of this kind, we want to know it now—not at the end of a year.

All family members receive monthly reports on how well their investments are doing. If things are working out well and everyone's happy, fine. If things aren't working out well, as sometimes they don't, we'll meet again and discuss what needs to be done. Also, sometimes the family situation changes. For example, the original purpose of a parent-child partnership may have been for capital growth, but now there is a need for income. The money manager that was selected may be an expert on growth strategies but knows less about producing income. Often, family members aren't aware of the subtle changes in their needs until, one day, they'll say, "That's right, I really think we have changed our criteria." Our monthly report and our quarterly meetings help jog this kind of thinking.

The whole process of locating, selecting, hiring and monitoring money managers is extremely satisfying for all family members, because this is usually the first time they have approached the question of money management from a rational and methodical standpoint. The sons and daughters feel greatly empowered because they have been given the freedom to make many choices. The parents are not only learning, themselves—they can see that their children are learning a process that will serve them well in the future. Once again the family has taken a giant step forward in preparing the children to inherit wealth and to manage it wisely.

1   The Family Business Program, Owner Managed Business Institute (OMBI), 226 East De La Guerra St., Santa Barbara, CA 93101

2   Bronfman, Joanie, Doctoral thesis, *The Experience of Inherited Wealth: A Social-Psychological Perspective*, UMI Dissertation Service, Ann Arbor, MI 48106

12 How You View Your Children

Do you believe that your sons or daughters will have the competence to handle your wealth? If they're like most children, yours have sometimes been irresponsible, and they have made many of the errors that are typical of young people. Has this made you doubt their maturity and judgment? Of course. But, overall, how objective is your opinion of them?

The time that an entrepreneurial parent spends away from home compounds the impression of children that are ill-equipped to handle wealth. A classic model of the entrepreneurial family unfolds something like this.

Dad, who is usually the family entrepreneur, comes home blustering because that is the way he runs his business—giving orders and expecting people to do as he tells them. Dad expects the children to have an adult level of competence because he is accustomed to that on a daily basis. To a lesser or greater degree, but always to some degree, the children are intimidated by their father even though they love and respect him. Because they don't get to see too much of him, they don't understand the rules by which he is playing, and how they should react. This undermines the children's confidence and lessens their *apparent* judgment skills in Dad's eyes.

Because she has spent so much time with them, from when they were little, Mom has a sensitive understanding of the children's abilities. She has been a part of the daily trials they have experienced; she's watched how they learned to deal with their peers and how they gradually became more responsible. Mom knows their strengths close-up, and the long, day-by-day struggle it has been for the children to attain them. So when Mom suggests to Dad that perhaps he is being a bit harsh, that maybe he is expecting too much and is missing some of their good points, Dad would do well to listen. While she may be instinctively downplaying some of the children's faults, she is providing a counter to Dad's critical nature.

Because the spouse of an entrepreneur is often inexperienced in business and money matters, the entrepreneur tends to disregard his or her spouse's input in evaluating the grown-up children's ability to manage wealth. Sometimes I'll ask an entrepreneur client, "What do you think of your spouse's ability to manage money and to evaluate your children as custodians of wealth?" The usual response is something like, "Not much." Then I ask, "How much time do you spend each month teaching your spouse how to manage money?" And the reply is, "What do you mean, teach money management?" Until we take up the subject, they have never even thought about this.

If Dad opts to keep his wife uninformed, and he disregards her insights about the children, he is losing a valuable perspective.

What I always recommend to Dad is that he begin teaching Mom about money management. The processes I mentioned in the previous chapter, such as family partnerships and a family bank, are good ways to do this. When Mom has learned some money-management skills, her input, together with Dad's, can achieve a proper balance and perspective in evaluating the children. In my experience, this balance works regardless of whether Dad or Mom is the entrepreneur.

When you have acquired a reasonable and balanced view of your grown-up children's strengths and weaknesses, how do you determine whether or not they are capable of handling wealth or of managing a business? One way *not* to determine this is by allowing your feelings of the moment to be the judge. Not only is that a poor way to decide—it isn't fair to them. Instead, I recommend to my clients that they begin to set up standards for their sons and daughters...something like a job description. For example, what formal education requirements, if any, do you want the children to have? What if your daughter has learned to be a competent money manager but doesn't want to go to college? Will you still require her to get a college degree before allowing her to inherit family wealth?

Some entrepreneur fathers tend to say, "I built my business without a formal education: my children can probably do the same."

Others, who regret their own lack of education (or who feel the lack of the prestige it confers), demand that their grown-up sons and daughters obtain MBA's.

What is more realistic is to look at the actual knowledge requirements for being able to control family wealth effectively, and to compare those requirements to the personality, aptitudes and desires of each son and daughter.

In setting up standards for their grown-up children, some entrepreneurs require a minimum amount of experience dealing with charities. This led to a conflict between one of my clients, George Seerlock, and his twenty-five year old son, Charles. The conversation went something like this:

At a family meeting, George said to his son, "I would like you to start spending a minimum number of hours each month working with charities."

"Well, Dad, I can't. I'm going twenty-six hours a day as it is. I don't have time for charities now—I'm fighting for survival in my own business."

"I know, son, but the distribution of several million dollars in charitable donations each year is a big part of what your family responsibilities will eventually be."

"Dad, how much time and energy did you give to charities when you were my age? When did you get active in charities? It was when you got to the point in your life when you had things under control and you had the time to think about it, right?"

"That's true, Charles, but now we're talking about a substantial family inheritance, and you have to understand that charitable activities are a part of the responsibilities of that inheritance. Do you understand what I'm saying?"

At that point I interrupted before the threats and ultimatums began flying back and forth. My input was to suggest and help set up a reasonable time frame for charitable involvement by George's son. After discussion, the family agreed that Charles would only have to attend quarterly family meetings on charitable activities over the next two years, so he would at least have some familiarity with what was happening. After that, his involvement would increase until, after ten years, he would be fully engaged with the family's charitable activities. This changed the debate from an emotional conflict to a practical plan. It set up specific, minimum requirements for George's son to begin to share the control of family assets if he wished.

In any family, there are bound to be disagreements between parents and their children over what education, life experiences and special skills are required before the young adults are competent to inherit and control wealth. With some families, the parents may insist that a liberal arts education and world travel are necessary before their children have the perspective to use wealth beneficially. In other families, actual job experience with several different companies is the main criterion.

The initial standards which are set up are not the most important thing. After all, standards can be changed if conditions and viewpoints change. First, establishing standards means that the family has tacitly agreed there should be some objective, specific way to determine whether or not the grown-up children are competent to receive and use wealth wisely. Standards also mean that the threat of disinheritance is no longer a weapon that can be arbitrarily wielded in order to assure good behavior and general compliance. Inheritance becomes a guarantee that is tied to specific goals which are reasonable and attainable, and for which sons and daughters can plan and strive. Finally, and most importantly, the standards become a starting point that stimulates family communication; this is a good opportunity for sons and daughters to express their views.

Some entrepreneurs try to control their children's behavior by use of the other Golden Rule: he who has the gold makes the rules. When the children are small, it usually shows up in control of smaller things, such as "If you're out past ten o'clock you lose your allowance!" When the children are grown, it may well involve larger issues, such as "You marry that nincompoop and you lose your inheritance!" In one classic case, the father said to me, "I'm not gonna give my daughter and her husband a penny because I don't like the - - ! I told her not to marry that guy. He's a - - - and I don't trust him!"

"How about the grandchildren?" I asked.

"They're the result of that - - union. To hell with them. I'm not gonna give them anything either!"

"You mean to tell me that your love is really that conditional? That you only love your daughter on the condition that she does what you say? Didn't you raise her to be independent?"

"Well, sure." he said.

"Congratulations," I said, "you succeeded. I can understand your not wanting to give anything to your son-in-law. Nothing in the world says you have to like him or give him anything. But do you mean to tell me you're going to cut your daughter off completely because she married the wrong guy? And look at your grandchildren. They had no choice in this, did they?"

"Well..." he said. He was softening a bit, and I continued.

"After you're dead, do you honestly think your wife is going to keep them cut off? If anything, she's going to try to give them twice as much because she feels so guilty. And who will benefit? Lawyers and the IRS. And who will be hurt? Your grandchildren, because there's going to be lawsuits and a lot of bitterness. Now come on, let's get on with what's real. We can structure things so that your money follows the line of descendency. Better yet, let's start educating your daughter and your grandchildren in how to manage money wisely, so that it will be a blessing and not a curse."

In Chapter 11, I discussed the problem of when to tell the children specific financial information about family wealth. In some cases a particular son or daughter, even when grown-up, still may not seem capable of receiving this information. But there is another side to this issue, and it is the deliberate withholding of financial information, as a tool to try to control children's behavior. Like the more blatant form of parental control, where arbitrary judgments and personal biases are causes for disinheriting children, the deliberate withholding of financial information causes one of two reactions in the children. Either they grudgingly comply with their parents' wishes and harbor a strong resentment against them, or they defy their parents, and both parents and children are resentful. Here are some examples from the grown-up children of wealthy parents.

"My father's been telling me if I want to look at the financial stuff any time now it's alright. I think he means it, but when I get there it's so complicated. I never get a direct answer of how much or anything like that."

"I'm struggling to get the information. I say, 'Tell me how much money I have.' They say, 'It's very hard to compute because so much of it is underground.' I say, 'I bet you compute it when you want a loan at the bank. I bet you can come up with the figures.'"[1]

The subtlest form of controlling children's behavior with money may be partly subconscious. The relationship between John Kolski and his grown-up daughter, Carla, illustrates this point.

Carla was starting her own real estate contracting company and she wanted to build a house. She approached her trustee and asked for a $150,000 loan.

The trustee told her, "I already released a million dollars to you last year."

"What are you talking about? I never received anything!"

"One million dollars was released to you. Go check with the accountant."

Carla went to the trustee's office. Sure enough, there was a record of a check written to her in the amount of one million dollars. Her father had *neglected* to tell her about it and had deposited it into a savings account because he didn't think she needed it and wasn't ready for it. *Carla is 38 years old and has four children.*

Whose money is it? Another client gave his son $250,000 to keep and to invest as he chose. The money belonged to the son, but his Dad kept close watch over it. "What have you invested in?" "Let me see your portfolio." "Can't you do more than 10 percent?" "Remember, I worked hard for that money." Finally, at a family meeting, his son said, "I don't want this money. It's still Dad's money. If I'm going to get any money, I want it to be *my* money."

Sometimes, the money remains Dad's money, even when that is not his intent. It's not uncommon to hear the wives of entrepreneurs say, "It's my husband's money, it's not my money. He earned it, I didn't." This is after thirty or forty years of marriage and the raising of a family.

Family partnerships and other family financial agreements have to be conditional—that is, the children (and parents) must adhere to the rules. But when parents *give* money to their children, it is important that there be no strings attached—legal or emotional. Their children have to be free to take risks with it as they see fit. Dad or Mom can advise, *when advice is requested,* but they have to allow their children freedom to risk, even if there is a possibility that the money will be partially or wholly lost. In practice, the hardest part is not convincing parents of this, but convincing their children that it really is their money, and that there are no emotional liens on it.

Trusts are ironically named, because they often indicate a lack of trust. They are also subject to misuse. This occurred in the family of Milton Pike. Milton founded and built up a large printing and binding business with fifty million dollars in annual sales. He had twin daughters, and he established a trust for the purpose of safeguarding his daughters' inheritance until they reached the age of twenty-one. But when the young women came of age, their father found ways to keep extending the trust. This angered and frustrated them. Finally, when they were both almost thirty years old and had still received nothing, they vented their resentment at their father. They asked, "When will we ever be mature enough, in your eyes, to handle money?" Finally, they hired a lawyer. After several years of litigation, the lawyer managed to break the trust, and the daughters received the money. But it left a legacy of terrible bitterness in the family which continues to this day.

Parents can usually think of several reasons to establish trusts for their children, such as waiting for their maturity, and protecting them from mistakes. Left unsaid is the desire to control their behavior and their lives in general. But controlling grown-up children and mistrusting their judgment can be a self-fulfilling prophecy—they aren't allowed to take risks, they can't learn from their mistakes, and they simply don't mature.

As a parent, it is very important to distinguish between wanting to see certain levels of maturity in your children, on the one hand, and forcing them to do what you think is "right," on the other. One idea that works well is to create performance-based trusts rather than age-based trusts. For example, instead of having a trust pay out at age twenty one, the first payment can be tied to graduating from college; the second payment might require five years job experience before payment, and so on.

Family offices often play a large role in trusts, regularly disbursing small amounts to mature adults. But place yourself in this position: how would you like to be fifty years old and still be receiving an "allowance?" But more than that, the family office provides exactly the wrong kind of psychology to the inheritor. It is saying, "We will safeguard your parents' money, and you needn't worry about it or be responsible for it." But what the inheritor really needs is for the family office to be a dynamic and creative partner, and to provide opportunities for growth and increasing competence with money.

The final point of this chapter is the importance of being forthcoming with your children about their inheritance. One client of mine decided to clear the air in this regard and, at a family meeting, he said to his three kids: "I love each of you too much to give you any money." This was a difficult position for him to take.

The children reacted strongly to this; they didn't like it. They felt they were being judged unfairly, and that they should have the right to prove themselves competent to receive family wealth. Their dad's decision may not stand forever. but it did one thing for sure: it made the children sit up and take notice. It was also a catalyst for family communication because there were numerous discussions from that point on.

I don't recommend disinheriting your children. On the contrary, I strongly believe that you should spend the next ten years educating your children to a high level of competence and positive values. If you do this, I guarantee your children will do a far better job of handling their money than if you leave their education to chance.

Much of this chapter has been about the degree of trust with which parents are able to view their children. Many of the recommendations, such as setting up standards for grown-up children and learning to give without attaching strings, are not easy for the entrepreneurial parent to do. In fact, as much as children have to learn to be trustworthy, Dad and Mom have to learn to give up a measure of control over them. So the question of whether or not your children, when they are grown-up, are really competent and worthy of inheriting family wealth, depends not only on what they do, but on what you do, as well.

1   Bronfman, Joanie, Doctoral thesis, *The Experience of Inherited Wealth: A Social-Psychological Perspective*, UMI Dissertation Service, Ann Arbor, MI 48106

13 Involving Your Family With Your Business

One form of parental control is for parents to make their children's inheritance contingent upon their working for the family business, without considering the children's talents and wishes. As I have said in previous chapters, the true blessing of money is that it provides options. An inheritance should do the same; it should enlarge the inheritors' freedom to pursue what *they* wish. While the family wealth does provide a wonderful opportunity for children who are inclined to business life, parental pressure on unwilling children to manage family interests invariably results in unfulfilled lifetimes spent trying to pursue someone else's vision.

On the other hand, a common theme among our clients is when a daughter wants to join the business but is prevented from doing so. This was the case with Leonard Hansen and his two sons and two daughters. The oldest daughter, Holly, was by far the most capable of the Hansen children from a business standpoint, but Leonard didn't believe that women should run a business. He used every excuse to avoid discussing this issue. When I became involved, neither Holly nor her younger sister were even part of the buy/sell agreement. It took an unbelievable amount of work to get Leonard and his two sons to acknowledge that Holly was a capable executive; that, at the least, she and her sister should have the option of owning stock in the company. Leonard finally agreed to give his daughters their one-fourth shares in the company upon his death, and that each of them would have a "put" to the company for their shares if they wanted to get out. Leonard still won't acknowledge what a great asset Holly is to his company, but we continue to work on him.

What happens when none of the sons or daughters are qualified or motivated to run the business? This is an instance where direct, truthful family communication is vital. When a son, on behalf of himself and his siblings, says to his father: "You know, Dad, none of us are really interested in running the business," that will hurt Dad in the short term. But it lets him know that in the long run he has to find a buyer for the business (or bring in other management with his children on the Board). This makes Dad's life easier because at least the air is cleared and he can plan the direction of the company in preparation for an eventual sale.

The decisions of grown-up children not to participate in the family business aren't cast in stone—they may change their minds when they are exposed to the world of business and its challenges and rewards. This is another reason why it is important to follow-up on the methods to promote their involvement which I suggested in Chapter 11, such as teaching your children money management and forming family partnerships and a family bank. These will make your children well disposed to participating in the family business if they have any aptitude for it at all. In my experience, if you begin this training early—when your children are in their 20's or earlier—there is a good chance they will want to come on board. If you wait until they are in their late 30's or their 40's, they will probably be past the stage where they are willing to abandon their own careers and learn what is necessary to run the business.

I find it very useful to have the grown-up children of my clients complete questionnaires about themselves and their attitudes toward the family business. I use a separate questionnaire for those sons and daughters who already have expressed a desire to work in the family business and for those who haven't. From the questionnaire for those who want to participate, here are a few samples of the questions asked: "Do you have a track record of managing other people successfully?" "Do you have a track record of guiding successful projects from conceptualization to completion?" "Are your assumptions and expectations about your role in the family business realistic?" "How would you anticipate providing security for your mother and father if and when they give up control?"

Here are a few sample questions from the questionnaire for sons and daughters who don't want to participate in the family business: "Do you know who could run the business if your father died today (or your mother, if she runs the business)?" "Will you be able to monitor the activities of those who manage the business?" "What do you think will happen to the company, money, assets and the family unit after your mother and father die?"

The purpose of these questions is to introduce topics which have typically been neglected or avoided. They encourage both parents and their children to discuss a wide range of issues, from attitudes toward the business to the parents' judgments of their children's abilities.

No matter how perceptive Mom or Dad are, they are so emotionally tied up with their children that it is almost impossible for them to be truly objective about their capabilities without outside help. In fact, the best way to evaluate young adults is to have them work for someone else. This gives the young person a different perspective and it demonstrates how an objective world values his labor. It also insures he won't receive special treatment or be absolved of responsibilities which other employees have.

After a few years of work experience, several things will have changed for the young adult. He knows he has to be worth what he gets paid, and if he has only been able to make $15,000 per year, that tells him he has more to learn. But if Dad says "I can only pay you $15,000," and his son has been able to command a salary of $40,000 per year, he can look Dad in the eye and say, "Sorry, I know what I am worth in the world, and if you aren't willing to pay that, I won't come to work for you." The work experience also allows him to speak with more credibility. If Dad says something that doesn't ring true, he can say with some confidence, "Sorry Dad, but I've seen the way that works and you're doing it the wrong way." The son is speaking to his father with credentials given to him by his experience in the business world. This elevates him in Dad's eyes (as well as in the eyes of non-family managers in the business) and it enables him to know he can make real contributions to the family business. If that son becomes an executive of the family firm, he can compare standards and methods against what he has seen in other companies, and that will make him a better executive.

When, for one reason or another, it isn't feasible for an entrepreneur's son or daughter to find other work, or when Dad sees that some specialized kind of work experience will be an advantage, mutually-beneficial arrangements can be made. Several of my clients have asked business friends to hire their son or daughter for a period of time, with two stipulations: 1) That the father will pay the salary until the son or daughter actually begins to earn it, and 2) That the child be treated and evaluated exactly as every other employee. This period of testing and tutelage in a friend's company often works so well that, after the training period, the friend is loathe to let the youngster go.

When a son or daughter is brought into the family business, it is important that clear standards be established. What are the educational and job experience requirements for the intended position? If it is to be Chief Financial Officer, is a CPA license and/or an MBA in finance required, and must he or she work for the company a certain number of years before receiving the CFO title?

Nepotism is a common problem with family-owned companies. An example of a classic case is related by Clive Cushman, who manages a large construction company in the Midwest. Clive was hired by the owner to be Division Manager, with authority to make all decisions for that division. But the owner has two sons and he is pushing to get them into the business. He wants his sons to have some supervisory experience and he has asked Clive to let them each be Assistant Managers directly underneath him.

The owner's sons are both capable young men, but they are not as knowledgeable and experienced as other employees in the company. Clive's problem is that if he agrees to let the owner's sons come in at top levels, what kind of a disincentive will that be for the more qualified employees who want those jobs? Also, Clive knows that the owner's sons will only be there a couple of years and then they will move on to start new divisions, leaving him short of trained managers.

If Clive caves in to the owner's demand. he knows that the other employees will resent having the two sons become instant managers, and morale and performance will drop. If Clive resists, he knows he'll be replaced sooner or later. It's a very difficult situation, and it points up the problems which occur when an owner's children are given special treatment.

Jennifer Ames has developed an interesting plan for her son and two daughters. Jennifer owns a large travel agency in Pennsylvania which she bought several years ago and has built up to thirty-two branch offices. Jennifer began by identifying eight key positions in her company, with definite requirements for each position. Even if all three of her children want to work in the company, there are enough top positions so that there is room for her other employees to advance, as well.

Jennifer wants to retire when she is sixty two—in about four years. She has enlisted three highly competent businesswomen to act as tutors to her son and daughters. Each tutor has been guaranteed the opportunity to buy into her company when Jennifer retires. The tutors, in turn, have agreed to teach her son and daughters all aspects of the travel business. Each sibling will work for a year with each tutor. At the end of three years, the tutors will give Jennifer their opinions on the competency of the son and daughters.

If at least two of the three opinions on a particular son or daughter are positive, that individual will be given the opportunity of selecting one of the available key positions in the company.

This plan accomplishes several things. It sets standards for Jennifer's children; it gives them broad work experience with three different companies, under expert guidance; it lets them know what they must do in order to get a management position in the family business; and, finally, it provides for an objective judgment of their capabilities.

In training grown-up children to work in the family business, most entrepreneurs forget to impart knowledge that they alone possess. Suppose for a moment that you are one of these typical entrepreneurs. From all of the years you have been in business, you have collected a storehouse of knowledge that is probably not written down anywhere. For example, is it documented anywhere that you have verbally promised the owner of Precision Parts, Inc. to deliver within 20 days of receipt of their order instead of within the thirty days called for in the contract? Or does anyone on your staff know that Frank Peabody has given you a ninety-day option to pick up that bargain property across town? This kind of informal knowledge includes all kinds of personal commitments to suppliers; agreements with customers; relationships with bankers; and various in-house procedures and operations. You haven't needed these things written down because you know them so well you take them for granted. But if something should happen to you, this knowledge—necessary information that enables the company to thrive—will be lost. Even if you remain active in the business, it will make your children's efforts to learn about the company much harder if they have to extract this information out of you drop by drop.

To help young adults understand how a business really works, and to avoid a possible disaster, I recommend that entrepreneurs begin to keep a log of informal business knowledge. One way the entrepreneur can do this is to keep a reminder on his desk to ask himself, after each telephone call or letter: "Is this something which I have exclusive knowledge about?" If so, he can enter the information into a logbook or into a computer file. This will be of tremendous benefit to his sons or daughters, or to whoever will be running the company in the future.

To briefly summarize the points in this chapter:

- Involving your children with family investment projects will predispose them to working with the family business.

- If, when your children are grown-up, they are interested in working for the family business, encourage them to work for someone else for a few years as preparation.

- Objective standards for your grown-up children, both for job requirements and job performance, help clear the air and avoid most of the problems of nepotism.

Your business provides your sons and daughters with wonderful opportunities that are not available to most youngsters. If you let them see the challenges, the opportunities and the rewards which accompany entrepreneurship, the chances are they will be willing and enthusiastic participants.

14 Planning for Succession

The founder of a family business is a unique breed of individual. He or she has demonstrated an abundance of creativity, initiative, determination, boldness, leadership and perseverance—the traits that are necessary to face the challenges of starting a business and building it until it has become a substantial enterprise. But the traits that are required to start and build a business are not necessarily the same as those required to maintain and expand one.

What kind of a business will yours be in the future? When you are no longer active, it is probably reasonable to say that your business will be in an expansion and maintenance phase, rather than in a building phase. The history of all the major corporations in the U.S. that have successfully passed from founder to the next generation shows that the heirs needed skills different from those of the founder. What are the skills that will be needed in your business of the future? Rather than independent initiative, perhaps those skills will be more oriented to computers, systems management and international trade regulations, to name a few. Are you helping your sons and daughters to acquire these skills?

Planning for your future business is *fundamentally different* from running your current business. In the future, *you* won't be around to respond to the needs of the business. So your planning must focus on developing the leadership skills of your children and any others who will be running your company. Developing leadership in others requires a far different skill than displaying leadership yourself. Further, because you won't be around to respond to specific problems, your planning for the future must include developing the kind of structure and tools that will best enable your heirs to respond to any problems which arise.

A succession plan is not the same thing as an estate plan, even though the two are interrelated. An estate plan determines how all of the family assets will be passed along to heirs and other beneficiaries. A succession plan determines how the family assets, including the business, will be managed and controlled. Typically, both plans are developed concurrently, because each affects the other.

A lack of planning for the future is often due not as much to shortsightedness as to reluctance to give up control. Time after time I have heard clients say that they're waiting for the *right time*, or that their grown-up children *aren't ready yet*. This is the case with John Phipps and his two sons. John grudgingly acknowledges that planning for the future is necessary, and he has agreed, in principle, that his two sons will take over his manufacturing business, but he refuses to take any steps to implement it. His two sons, who are now in their late 40's, have been made vice-presidents in the company but, in reality, they have no power or authority. When they make decisions, their father sometimes reverses them. The sons are terribly frustrated and are at the point of leaving the company.

John started his company on a shoestring, and one of his most striking attributes has been his dogged independence, which has served him well up to now. Like many another entrepreneur, he feels that he alone has the insight to make things work and that he alone is ultimately responsible for the welfare of the business. John's natural self-confidence deludes him into believing that his past success automatically assures his success in the future. John is in his 70's and he has lost much of his entrepreneurial energy. At this time in his life, he isn't really interested in developing new products and new markets, while his sons, who are in their prime, want to follow what they perceive as good opportunities. Yet their father never asks for their advice and he doesn't receive it kindly when it is offered. John is not only about to lose his sons' services, he has already lost their love and respect. Family meetings are confrontational and angry, without any prospects for change. The company, which had been doing eighty million dollars in annual sales, has consistently been losing market share for the past three years, and sales are down. It is a classic case of the aging and stubborn entrepreneur refusing to face reality, and losing his company and his children as a result.

If John Phipps was able look at his situation objectively, he would see that he badly needs to develop a succession plan. He needs to begin a program of transferring his broad skills and knowledge to his sons, while he is still around to do it. A founder who is easing up on control doesn't need to give up all business activities—there are several important functions he can continue to do for the company, as he allows his children more responsibility in running it. But perhaps the hardest lessons for the mature founder to learn is that his own ideas must now be subject to collaboration instead of being simply implemented at his orders, as before. The contribution of skills and knowledge now become a two-way street; the founder's experience and knowledge continue to guide his children, but the newer, up-to-date viewpoints they have acquired are also valuable. The mature founder, who is gradually giving up control of his company, will realize that his strongest contribution is not his continuing day-to-day activity but his role as mentor.

There are many psychological reasons why entrepreneurs and their families resist talking about Dad giving up control of the business. Dad resists because he can't deal with letting go. His whole identity may be based on the business so that he feels lost without it. And the whole subject reminds him of his mortality. Mom and the children don't like to bring up the subject of Dad's easing out because it's uncomfortable for them to speak openly of his eventual retirement and death. It's also awkward for the grown-up children to discuss taking over the business because to talk about it seems callous, and they don't want to hurt Mom and Dad's feelings. Even employees of the company (including those who complain about "management") don't like to think about the owner departing because it means changes and a less-certain future with the company.

Here is where the skilled facilitator can make a real difference. At a family board meeting, I may start out by saying, "We have not covered the issue of what happens when Dad dies; what it will mean to everyone if the business is retained, merged or sold. If Dad dies before Mom (and I say this while Dad is sitting there), is it reasonable that all of the money goes to Mom until her death?"

In the particular family I'm thinking of, Mom is forty-eight years old, and the two sons, by Dad's former marriage, are forty-three and forty-six. The discussion continues with my next statement, addressed to the two sons, Peter and Ken.

"Now assume your Dad has left everything to both of you, but statistically speaking, your Mom is going to outlive you. Do you know how much of the inheritance you are going to get? Nothing. How do you feel about that?"

"Well," Ken said, "we don't have any choice in the matter. Whatever they want to do, they'll do."

"That's right," I said, "but let's assume you and your brother do have a choice and you get to have some input in the matter. Should you both have to pay Dad's estate taxes, should we find a way that is less painful, or will you both decide to liquidate the company in order to pay the taxes?"

I've introduced several rhetorical questions at this point. I'm not looking for answers yet, I just want to get some of these topics on the table. "Peter, let's say that you are going to be running the company and you're going to be earning half a million dollars a year.

And you, Ken, will only be getting fifty thousand a year as a dividend, if Peter pays a dividend, which is unlikely, because that's double taxation. So you're probably going to get nothing. What do you think about that? Peter is running the company and earning half a million from your assets— from the half that you own. After Dad is gone, do you think some resentment might creep in? Would you, at some point, be tempted to say to Peter, 'I want my share. Even if I only put it in the bank, I'd get a five percent return. You're not even paying me that!'"

Meanwhile, Dad is sitting there, grinning and really enjoying this. The family has never discussed any of this before, and he is very interested in what the boys think. I continue. "How can we resolve this? Does it seem right that you, Ken, are locked into company ownership without any income? Or maybe you'd like to work for the company, too. As what? Janitor, president or vice-president? If you want to be president, are you qualified? Or put it this way: if you owned the company, would you hire someone with your present qualifications to be president? No, of course not. But who do you think is the best qualified person to run the company? Anyone here? No. So what is going to happen to the company if nobody is qualified to run it? Is it just going to flounder and die?"

Dad is listening, and he would love to hear the answers to all of these questions (which we will get to during the course of these meetings). Everyone in the family senses this is a very important time; that this is something which needs doing. I continue the discussion on a different tack.

"If Dad dies and you, Peter and Ken, are both running the company, what is Mom going to live on? Let's assume that the company is generating "X" amount of money and Mom needs more than that. How are you going to pay her? She's not working for the company, is she? Can we put her on the payroll anyway? No, because that's illegal. If you need to pay Mom a quarter of a million dollars a year, it's going to cost you another $160,000 in taxes. So you'll need about $400,000 to do it. Her income is construed as a dividend; Mom will have to pay taxes on her quarter of a million. Double taxation. Does that make sense?"

Dad is smiling. From his business experience, he knows the answers and what to do, but his sons don't. Now they are starting to realize how much they don't know. As the discussion goes on in this vein, I make the sons work at coming to grips with what they think is fair, what they want to do, and how they are going to do it. Then I turn to Mom and continue:

"How secure do you feel about receiving income after Dad is gone? If one or both of the sons are going to run the company, do you feel confident of their abilities to keep it going? Or would you feel safer hiring more experienced persons, not in the family, to run the company? But that shuts out Peter and Ken. Is that fair to them? Remember, your future is on the line here. Are you willing to risk your income for the rest of your life on them? If not, what would you want to happen before they take over the company? Or would you want to work for the company yourself? If yes, are you qualified?"

Hard questions, all of them. And Mom is uncomfortable because she is being placed in an awkward situation. But these are matters the family must deal with in planning for succession. If these candid give-and-take discussions are avoided, succession can become a crisis, especially when precipitated by the unexpected death of an entrepreneur.

This happened when a friend of mine was tragically killed one night in an auto accident. For all the years he was married, he had never told his wife, Fran, anything about his business—and she never inquired. Fran had been a wonderful wife and mother, but she knew nothing about finances, not even her own checking account.

After her husband's sudden death, Fran sought refuge with friends. They were good people who were looking out for her, but they knew nothing about business. They told her: "Watch out for your husband's partner. After a partner dies, that's when the other partner takes advantage of the widow." That advice, together with the shock of her husband's death and her anxiety over her financial situation, caused Fran to panic. She began coming to the office each day and questioning the secretaries: "What are you doing? Let me see that," and she would pull the letters out of typewriters and read them. Fran took the company books home for months at a time, even though she couldn't interpret them, in order to give the impression that she couldn't be cheated. Her husbands's partner was going out of his mind. Finally, he obtained a court order to get the books back, just to keep up the accounts.

Fran continued this kind of behavior, disrupting company board meetings with irrelevant challenges and mistrusting everyone, trying to oversee things she knew little about. One day the remaining partner said to me, "Roy, what am I going to do with her? I'm not cheating her, she's my partner's wife for chrissakes! I'll buy her out and give her all the money I have. I can't stand any more of this." He was right—he couldn't. The strain on him was too much, and he succumbed to a stroke. Without either experienced partner at the helm, the company plummeted and was eventually forced into bankruptcy.

Fran and her husband had a son and two daughters. The effect of all this on them was catastrophic. In addition to dealing with the death of their father, the children had seen the world of business through their mother's eyes, and they are growing up scared and mistrustful of everyone. Fran wasn't unintelligent—her husband could have taught her the basics of business and money management. He could have asked several of his business friends to act as an advisory board to his wife in case something happened to him. Imagine how different Fran's life would have been, after her husband's death, if she had been able to gather together his trusted and knowledgeable friends, and say: "Advisers, help me get through this crisis. Tell me what to do."

An advisory team of experienced businessmen or businesswomen to counsel the surviving spouse and children of an entrepreneur is so helpful and effective that I now recommend this to my clients, almost without exception. If they wish, each member of the advisory board can pledge to be part of the advisory team for another member's spouse. In this way, it is mutually beneficial for all participants.

The entrepreneur can approach succession as a planned or an unplanned event. The planned event means that he sees himself gradually and voluntarily relinquishing responsibilities for the business, and managing the increasing involvement of his children. Some date in the future has been decided upon for the total transition. The unplanned, or crisis event, means that the entrepreneur intends to actively work in the business and to maintain control until—because of bad health or death—he cannot. At that point, his heirs must be ready to jump in and take command.

The planned succession allows a healthy transition from founder to heirs. Implicit in this planning is an open, cooperative family environment where all family members are invited to discuss succession issues and to air out their differences. Planning cannot be done by the founder alone—it must involve family members and outside advisers when needed. The real challenge of effective succession planning is for the whole family to be prepared for whatever events may occur.

The decisions that are arrived at through succession planning are extremely varied. To enable one or more siblings to get out of the family business, a funded, buy-sell agreement may be made, or a second-to-die contract may be created to pay estate taxes. The family may decide to have insurance on Dad, in order to pay the estate-tax bill or to buy out other partners if they want to leave the company.

Security for the parents is an important part of succession planning. Mike Jacobs, who is a client of mine, and his wife Edna, brought this up in a recent meeting. Mike and Edna are both in their late 50's, and they have two sons who want to take over the family lumber mill. Mike said to me, "Roy, if we turn the company over to the kids, they may take it down the tubes in ten years. In ten years, I'll be sixty-eight and Edna will be sixty-six—we may have another twenty years to go. What do we do then? It'll be too late to go back into the company." And Edna said, "We've spent our whole lifetime building up the company. We took lots of risks along the way. Now, I want some security. I want to sell the company."

Sometimes, the best answer *is* to sell the company. If that is the chosen course, the family should start looking for a buyer now, so it is not a crisis sale after Dad's death. There is absolutely nothing wrong with Dad and Mom deciding to sell the company *now* for the largest price they can get, and using the proceeds to really enjoy life. Whether the family decides that the business is to be retained, merged or sold, the common theme is still advance planning.

Taxes are very relevant to the issue of planning. The IRS tax code has divided the people who own wealth from the people who will inherit it. Now, Mom and Dad still have the assets—in this case, the business— but the estate has the responsibility for paying taxes on it—and the children, as inheritors, are many times unaware of the extent of this liability. Here's an example, using the case of Hugh and Emy McDowell, and their three children. The McDowell company is worth about three hundred million dollars. If Dad or Mom dies, all of the estate is passed on to the spouse, tax-free. That's wonderful! "No problems," Hugh tells his children, "There's nothing to worry about. We've got seven law firms and six accounting firms. Every document needed has been drawn up. It is all taken care of."

Now if Hugh should die, the scenario will look like this. Emy gets all of the three hundred million estate. If she receives a 5% return after taxes, that's fifteen million dollars a year. That is more than enough to keep her in the style to which she is accustomed. Time passes, and the grown-up children are now in their late 40's when Mom dies. The business has appreciated; the estate is now worth seven hundred million dollars.

The children seem set for life; they have inherited a seven hundred million dollar business. But now the IRS says: "We want four hundred million in cash for taxes. Oh yes, if you qualify under certain rules for closely-held assets, we will allow you to spread the payment over a period of time, but you will pay principal plus the prime interest rate. If you are late one day on the payments, it all becomes due and payable that day. The principal payment will be forty million per year, and the interest payment will be another forty million. We want eighty million dollars per year or we want the whole thing now—in cash."

A seven hundred million dollar business is a substantial asset. But have you ever tried to take cash out of a business? It's like squeezing all the juice out of an orange so that the only thing left is the rind and some pulp. How long can a company survive with fifty-five percent debt against assets and all the cash gone?

This is how the tax system works. The lawyers and accountants know it, and Mom and Dad know it. It's their children who are unaware. One of the questions that this raises is: do parents at least have the obligation to inform their children of the liability of the estate which they will inherit? If they are unprepared, this extraordinary liability will cause profound suffering and bitterness in the lives of their children. There are other options, and one of the tasks of the facilitator is to get the whole family together to look at them. If parents could look into the future and see how much potential pain that liability can cause their children, there is no doubt they would take the necessary steps to avoid it.

Another common problem I work on with my clients is how dilution of ownership begets lawsuits. The founder of a business is intimately close to that business. That intimacy is split when his two, three or four children inherit the business, and further divided when there are about eighteen grandchildren and, eventually, fifty or sixty great grandchildren, who all own shares.

When ownership is divided, it is often accompanied by a decrease in interest and knowledge about the business. If, for example, a grandchild owns one-ninth of the family business but is not actively involved in running it, how much loyalty to the business will he or she have? Will it be enough to allow the business to grow while he or she receives little or no return from that ownership? That is unlikely. More typically, the child or grandchild of the founder says, "I'm not getting anything for my share. I want to see some money."

How knowledgeable about the business will these one-ninth owners be? They are unaware of expansion plans, capitalization needs and possible negative cash flow. Their *apparent* interests no longer coincide with those of the business. The interests of the founder's grandchildren *who are running the company* are in opposition. They're trying to keep it going and to maintain their livelihoods at the same time. When push comes to shove, the lawsuits begin, and they can be very messy and very expensive.

In one case, a son and daughter and nine cousins were all shareholders in the family business. There was no really important strife between them—just the typical petty conflicts which are common in families. But each shareholder had his own lawyer, his own CPA and his own trust department at the bank. They were trying to run a huge company, but each time a decision had to be made, and one lawyer backed it, some of the other lawyers had to find some fault with it. The company never expanded because most of its profits were spent on legal fees. Sometimes, this is taken to extreme. In one well-publicized case, the family shareholders were dissatisfied with the company's performance and they fired the grandchild of the founder, who was running the company. He filed lawsuits against them, they counter-filed and, to date, both sides have spent twenty-three million dollars in legal fees. They have been fighting each other for years now, and there is no end in sight.

Another area of potential conflict is with in-laws. Pre- and post-nuptial agreements are helpful documents for families, but it is a challenge to create and implement agreements that avoid long-term conflicts. When someone asks their betrothed to sign a document in case they get divorced in the future, it sends a potentially contentious message. The reaction to it may be: we aren't even married yet and you are planning for our divorce. Here are some points to follow that help reduce the emotions which come with nuptial agreements.

1) Make it a family policy that everyone signs a nuptial agreement as a tool to protect family partners and family business interests.

2) Reassure spouses-to-be that the family does not think a divorce is going to occur, and explain the reasons for the family nuptial policy.

3) Give spouses-to-be adequate financial information so there are no secrets.

4) If you have a facilitator, discuss nuptial policy at a family meeting and make sure all spouses and spouses-to-be are invited.

5) Inform spouses-to-be of family nuptial policy at an early date, and don't wait until the last minute to ask them to sign.

6) Inform spouses-to-be that their future will be affected by the nuptial agreement, and that they should have their own lawyer to advise them.

Conflict among heirs over ownership or succession is not inevitable. One of my clients, Jeff Liguori, pursued an intelligent, reasonable and effective solution to succession in his company.

Jeff's business is manufacturing adult games like "Monopoly" and "Scrabble" for the game companies. He owns three printing and manufacturing plants. Some years before Jeff was ready to retire, he began to think about a successor. He had a bright young son-in-law who was untested; there was the possibility of a nephew and a niece; and there were also two key, female executives employed with the firm. They were all good, competent people, but he couldn't make a decision. So Jeff opted for a simple but innovative solution. He gathered all of the candidates together and asked them if they would try, by themselves, to form a succession team.

The mission of the five-member team was not only to choose an eventual CEO, but for each member to gain a familiarity with all aspects of the business, so that all of them would be in a position to perform needed, supporting roles. It took them two years. Gradually, the team acknowledged that the outstanding leader was the senior female executive. They took another year to confirm their choice by making her acting CEO and monitoring her performance, while Jeff remained in an advisory capacity. It was a terrific win-win situation for all participants. The team worked together so well that they decided to stay intact as a management advisory group, and Jeff was assured of not only a competent successor, but an effective support team.

One of the critical times in the transition of control from founder to successor is when the founder disagrees with a major decision of his designated successor. This is the make-or-break point of the succession. If the founder attempts to rescind his successor's decision, he will probably, at the least, lose the support of his successor; at the most, his successor will initiate a battle over control or will walk out.

For an entrepreneur who is planning for succession, it is necessary to put all of the cards on the table. At a meeting of the family board on the topic of succession, I will usually ask Dad: "When are you going to retire (I have already asked him in private, weeks prior to the meeting)? What will it take for you to feel comfortable that whoever you choose to run the company is competent? What experience level are you going to require that individual to have? Is there a family member or company executive you feel has the potential to run the company? If not, how are you going to find someone? If your son or daughter is going to be president of the company, do your employees know this? Have you discussed this decision with all of your key executives and advisers? Will your executives be comfortable with your choice of successor?"

When a succession plan has been developed and everyone has agreed to it, I request a meeting of the Family Advisory Board with all outside advisers present. Then I announce that this is a Succession Fire Drill, and that Dad has just "died" (while he is sitting there, watching). I want to know what the family board is going to do. Then I sit back, along with Dad, and take notes.

This is a foolproof way of finding out the flaws in the succession plan, seeing if everyone knows his or her responsibilities, and determining how well the plan is being implemented. It may take some time for this exercise to be completed, or we may run through it several times before everyone has it right. By then, Dad will have gained the confidence that the succession plan will actually work, because he has seen it work.

Sometimes, an adviser will be seen to be unprepared, or not to have done his job. I had one client who was outraged when he discovered, during a fire-drill exercise, that the work he had long ago requested had never been done. He fired his lawyer and his accountant the day after the exercise. The Succession Fire Drill is a tremendously powerful tool to test succession planning. I recommend it to *all* my clients and to *all those persons who believe they do not need to look into these issues.*

Succession planning takes time; it is not an overnight affair. It requires the continuing input of all family members, all close advisers and key personnel of the business. It also requires forthright, open communication. Succession planning is a way of anticipating possible future events and predetermining their outcome to the largest possible degree. It is a vital step in the process of preparing your children to inherit wealth.

15 Teaching your Family to Deal with Professionals

I recently read that an estimated three hundred thousand pages are being added to the Federal Register each year. That's just federal law and doesn't include state, county and municipal legislation and all of the court decisions at every level. This means there are literally millions of new laws on the books each year. There is no way that you (or I) can keep abreast of how these laws impact on your business. We need specialists—those who focus on relatively narrow areas such as business law and tax law. And so you have a team of specialists on call to assist you.

You rely on your attorney for legal matters, on your accountant for tax and audit matters, and on your technical people inside the company for specialized knowledge. But do you blindly accept and implement their advice without thinking it through yourself? No, of course not. You use these advisers as resources to help *you* make decisions. But what would happen if you weren't around? Would your spouse or your children be able to use this advice as effectively?

Our experience indicates that when the primary decision-maker of the family dies, the family will look for guidance to advisers whom they deem to be either more experienced or smarter. Often, they'll take the will, the buy/sell agreement and other documents to their lawyer and ask, "What do we do now?" The lawyer, looking at things from a legal standpoint, will give them a legal opinion. Your lawyer is not hired to recommend sound business decisions; he or she may not know if a given legal opinion is also a good business decision. This is true for most experts because, by definition, an expert has a particular focus.

An often-overlooked distinction is the difference between actual estate planning and drafting documents for an estate plan. Many lawyers are expert at drafting documents, and the prevailing view is that someone who produces good documents also produces a good plan. This is often not the case. Many well-drafted documents embody ineffective or inappropriate plans. Therefore, when you ask for an expert's opinion, someone has to take that opinion and place it in the broader context of the business and personal needs of family members. Someone has to determine exactly the areas in which that expert excels.

If something should happen to you, the business decision-maker in the family, it's likely that your family members will surrender their authority to a set of credentials—CPA, CFO or VP—and blindly accept an expert's advice. After all, you've often said to your family, "I'll talk to my lawyer about that," but you have never revealed to them the fact that you evaluate and sometimes challenge what the lawyer says. You haven't said to your spouse and children, "Here is what my advisers told me and, as a consequence, I am going to do this but I am not going to do that." The result of all of this is that the family believes that Dad does whatever his advisers tell him; and they follow suit and literally give up their authority and responsibility for their own future. This is often a dreadful mistake, and the family may pay the price for years to come.

When legal issues are involved, as they almost always are, it is helpful to understand the nature of the adversarial system. The responsibility of your lawyer is to protect your rights, not necessarily to resolve conflicts through nonlegal means. If he or she doesn't protect your rights, your lawyer may be liable. Therefore, if a lawsuit occurs, your lawyer will try to make sure that every word, every phrase and every detail is aired in court. This is what our adversarial system demands. The law firm, in order to be certain your rights are legally protected and that it can't be held liable for mistakes or poor representation, may carry the case to the "nth" degree, with cost as a secondary priority. Of course, in doing this, the law firm will make money. In fact, the monetary gains of the law firm, on the one hand, and protecting your rights, on the other, have become so intertwined that it is difficult to separate them. *The most important thing to understand from this is that a lawyer's method of protecting your rights is sometimes not in your best interest.* Case histories are replete with examples of companies failing because of well-intended but poor advice from professionals who are competent within their field, but who have no understanding of business or of the personal needs of the family.

I recall the case of Winnie Myers and her two sons. Winnie's husband had died two years earlier. For years, he had talked to his advisers alone and had never included other family members in these discussions. After he died, the older son stepped in to try to manage the company. In doing so, he incurred a debt of nine hundred thousand dollars and he was having trouble repaying it. After being served with a notice of default on the loan, Winnie went to her attorney, a very bright, competent man, and asked, "What can we do about the debt?"

"It's going to court," he said. "You signed a continuing guarantee and the bank has filed suit to collect on it. You don't have a choice."

From the legal viewpoint, her lawyer was right. And the suit was justified from the viewpoint of the lawyer representing the bank. But is it in the best interest of the family to settle the lawsuit out of court or not?

For some lawyers, their sincere perception is that the courtroom is the fairest and easiest way to resolve conflict, and courtrooms are where they can practice their art and earn their livelihood. But my experience tells me that the very last thing you want to do is go to court. My experience tells me that what is needed is for all the parties to sit down together and negotiate. When I became involved, I was able to get the family and the bank officers to sit down together. When all the facts were on the table, it became apparent that Winnie's company had been a good customer of the bank for a long time and that the company was basically sound. These were factors which hadn't been obvious from the legal documents. In just forty-five minutes, we were able to agree to dismiss the lawsuit and to negotiate payments in such a way that the family business could continue and the bank would feel secure about their loan.

The specialized focus of professionals was clearly spelled out for me when I attended a summer program at the Harvard Law School some years ago. In a class on estate planning, the professor told us that if we had questions, we were to submit them after class and he would address them the following day—he had too much material to teach us to allow interruptions during class time. But by the end of the first week, I had submitted about twenty-five questions and none of them had been addressed. I was exasperated.

When class began in the following week, I stood up and said, "Professor _____, I submitted twenty-five questions last week but none of them have been answered. Can you tell me when you will be able to address them? They are important to me." He glared at me and said, "You're Mr. Williams, aren't you?"

"Yes, sir," I said.

The professor turned to the rest of the class and said, pointedly, "Mr. Williams is *not* a lawyer." Then he turned back to me. "Mr. Williams, I want you to know that your questions have nothing to do with law—they have to do with business matters. They are business questions. If you have business questions, go to the business school. This is a course on law, and that is what we are discussing—not business."

"Professor _____," I replied, "I feel that my questions are relevant because the legal points you are citing would impact my clients."

He responded with: "Mr. Williams, if you insist on continuing this line of discussion, I'll have to ask you to leave this course. This is a law school not a business school, and this course has *nothing to do with business*."

The professor was absolutely, one hundred percent correct. What he was talking about was how to interpret the legal significance of a document. The business impact had nothing to do with it. When a businessman talks to his lawyer, he mistakenly believes that the lawyer is always talking about business. But he may not be. The lawyer may not have been trained in business and has no basis for talking about business—what he knows is his area of expertise. He may not be trained to think of new solutions to traditional problems. What I really learned from that Harvard law course is that when I talk to a lawyer, I am very much aware that we are discussing law. Since then, I ask lawyers or accountants to give me advice, based on their experience, about my options. I do not ask them to make decisions about business, family or personal matters.

When a family has lost its major businessperson and decision-maker, professional advisers can be very intimidating to the other members of the family. I see this happen time and time again to the families of my clients. The situation is exacerbated when the professionals at a family office tell family members, "You don't have to worry about that—we'll take care of everything." By relieving family members of responsibility, the family office is also keeping them ignorant and powerless. I feel strongly that professional advisers should be helping to educate the grown-up children of entrepreneurs, instead of isolating them.

Arthur Britten's family illustrates this point. Arthur owns several carpet mills in Georgia and North Carolina. For years, he has deliberately included his son and his daughter in his sessions with advisers. The son and daughter have watched how Dad deals with them, how he challenges them and how he evaluates their advice. About three years ago, Arthur had a chance to increase the vertical penetration of his market by acquiring a chain of retail carpet stores. It seemed to be a good deal. Arthur's son and daughter were there when Arthur's advisers and the selling parties got together for a presentation. Arthurs's MBA business consultant said, "We believe the numbers in this case are right, and the net profit of this venture will be a 20% compound return." Arthur's CFO supported this position.

His adult children, by this time, were experienced in dealing with advisers, and they watched and listened closely. When the presentation was over, they approached Arthur in private, and his daughter said, "Dad, there is something wrong with these numbers. We don't know what it is, but it's there. They are hiding something." They discussed it further and, although the money was on the table, Arthur decided to back off from the deal. Later, he found out that much of the information presented was fraudulent—even though the accountants had approved it—and the retail chain was in deep trouble.

Arthur's children had watched their father deal with advisers for several years. They saw him talk with the banker, the accountant, the lawyer and all the vice presidents, and how he challenged them all. From this they developed an intuitive sense of how their father used his advisers, and they came to understand the limitations of these advisers. The children had learned how their dad measures things, what he looks for and how he identifies the critical issues. They had learned to listen carefully to advisers, but to reserve judgment for themselves. In this particular case, these lessons were of real value, and they saved the family business millions of dollars by identifying a fraudulent deal.

There is no question that lawyers, accountants, insurance specialists, bankers and other professionals provide a needed resource for the entrepreneur. Too often, the entrepreneur regards these specialists as his personal resource and does not include other family members in his discussions with them. This isolation would not only be to the disadvantage of the family but to the disadvantage of the entrepreneur as well. When the entrepreneur meets alone with advisers and they identify a potential problem, it is far easier for him to deny the seriousness of that problem and to avoid corrective action than if other family members are present. I have worked with several clients who have been meeting alone with their advisers for years, and who have yet to come up with succession plans. This neglect would be hard to sustain if all family members were participants.

Advisers are trained to react to your needs in terms of their specialized solutions—they are not necessarily trained as decision-makers. Unless prodded, they may not dig for all the available options. How will your spouse and children gain your own ability to deal effectively with advisers? How will they learn that they don't have to accept advice simply because it comes from a set of credentials? They learn that by watching you work with your advisers, and seeing how you evaluate advice—sometimes accepting and sometimes rejecting it.

16 Projecting the Results of Succession

As a business matures, the kinds of skills required to manage it effectively change. Where the founder once needed traits such as bold risk-taking and the ability to locate opportunities and move quickly with them, the skills needed for the post-succession business may be quite different. In the future, the business may require expert management in such areas as employee benefit packages, environmental regulations, computer systems, international marketing, and so on. Identifying as many as possible of the skills which will be needed in the future to manage the business and other family assets, is a task that needs to be done now.

Who are the possible choices to manage your business in the future? Do these choices include your spouse, your children, or your key executives? What are the strong and weak points of each individual? If you have one successor in mind, do you have an alternate to take his or her place if needed? Are most of the needed skill/experience areas covered and, if not, can you initiate a training program to prepare your successors for management and improve their weak areas?

Matching the capabilities of your grown-up children, or other potential successors, to the needs of the future business is one step toward determining who will manage your business in the future.

Another is to try to assess how control and/or ownership of your business will affect the lives of your children. In this regard, one of the issues I raise with all of my clients is the difference between treating your sons and daughters *fairly* and *equally*. This is an important point, and I will illustrate it with an anecdote about your two mythical children, Johnny and Janey.

From the time they were very small you, as a loving parent, tried to treat your children fairly. And because they demanded it ("That isn't fair, Dad—Janey got one and I didn't!"), when one child got a new toy the other child had to have one as well. When you found time to play with Janey, you had to make time to play with Johnny. When you went out to the ice cream parlor, they both had to have the same size ice cream cone even though Johnny was much bigger, with a correspondingly larger appetite.

When Janey showed an aptitude for music and started piano lessons, you and your spouse probably felt guilty until Johnny was also receiving lessons, even though he didn't display the same musical talent. In money matters, did you give the children equal allowances (or equal amounts, based on their age) even though Johnny spent his as fast as he got it while Janey cautiously saved hers? Like most parents, you probably treated your children as equally as possible because the children, themselves, demanded it and because, most of the time, it seemed that *equal* treatment was *fair* treatment. Sometimes there were exceptions. For example, when Johnny made the football team and needed a uniform, cleated shoes, and pads, you didn't run out and get the same things for Janey.

Most of the time these decisions were fairly easy to make, based on common sense and the needs of the moment. But sometimes these kinds of decisions can be more complicated. For example, if Johnny was involved in an auto accident and incurred $100,000 in medical bills which weren't covered and for which you ended up having to pay—would you feel obligated to give Janey $100,000? No, probably not. But would you consider reducing Johnny's inheritance by $100,000? Probably not, you say, because it was an act of fate and not Johnny's fault. But what if it was proved that the accident was caused by Johnny's reckless driving? Would that affect your decision? In terms of their respective inheritances, what is *fair*?

Let's advance the time frame a few years. Johnny and Janey have grown up. John has been running your company for about ten years and has done a good job—he deserves to be president. Jane is not active in the business but she is a wonderful daughter. On several occasions, when your wife was ill, Jane left her own family to come and care for her, selflessly. You love both of your children very much, and you set up their inheritance so each will receive half of all assets.

More time passes and your adult children now own the company. John still runs it. He has a satisfying career and a substantial salary. The company is growing, profits are being reinvested and, because of this, no dividend is being paid. Jane has no quarrel with her brother running the company and getting adequate compensation for doing it, but she and her husband are having money problems. Jane knows that the company is now worth thirty million dollars and, although she owns half of it, she is not receiving anything. She wants her share or, at least, she wants the income she could get from fifteen million dollars. The company can't generate that kind of cash and John and Jane can't agree on what to do, so lawsuits are filed. The courts finally force liquidation of the company, and both children's families part with what appears to be permanent bitterness. All your years of effort and your hope that the company will continue to flourish—all disappear in a cloud of rancor and a family divided.

This is not a fanciful projection—I've seen it happen time after time. But it doesn't have to be this way. The solution is available; it is to create a far-sighted succession plan that treats each sibling *fairly*, anticipating their future needs and desires. It also means explaining the plan openly to all of the children and, if they are married, to their spouses.

Let's return to John and Jane, now having grown up and inherited your business. Your far-sighted succession plan included sufficient liquidity to fund a binding buy/sell agreement (which we can call a "put"). This "put" now enables Jane, should she choose, to sell all or part of her share with a predetermined payment schedule which will not threaten the company. In this way, both John and Jane win, and the company continues to prosper. Your succession plan has also considered John's and Jane's children, and has established criteria for any of them who want to enter the business. It includes job descriptions, educational requirements and compensation levels. Because of this, your grandchildren all know where they stand and can consider their opportunities without envy of each other.

One of my tasks as facilitator is to look into the future and point out aspects of succession that result in fair or unfair treatment. These considerations then need to be addressed in open communication by the Family Advisory Board, until there is a consensus on what constitutes fairness. The final result is a succession plan that goes beyond the concept of equality and which is perceived by *all* as fair.

Another necessary element in an effective succession is for all members of the family to understand and respect the distinction between ownership, control and benefits. When understanding and respect for these are absent, trouble isn't far away. For the founding entrepreneur there is little need to acknowledge the distinctions—you manage your business, you own it and you gain the rewards from it. But for the spouse or children, the distinctions are important. This was a real problem for Jack Lamb. Jack had created a succession plan that gave 50% of his company to his wife, Jeanne, in the event of his death. It was hard enough to get Jack to do that because he didn't like thinking about his own mortality. Although I pressed him to explain to his wife the responsibilities and limits of company ownership, he never did.

It was left like that for many years. When Jack died, Jeanne had no idea what her role as a company owner should be. She had dearly loved her husband and she wanted to do her best to maintain the company he had built up over the years. Because her lawyer advised an assertive stance, Jeanne overcompensated for her naivete by trying to exert control over company operations. Jeanne is now a member of the Board of Directors and, although she can't legally control day-to-day company operations, her constant interference in them is making life miserable for management.

Jeanne has no idea of what is required to sustain the profitability of a large company. In fact, two of her key managers have become fed up and have quit. Market share and profits are declining and, due to this, coupled with the loss of the top managers, the value of the company has slid considerably. Jeanne, in spite of her good intentions, is ruining a fine company. Of course, by now she has been repeatedly told by her managers that ownership doesn't mean control, *but she has never been told that by anyone whom she completely trusts.*

If Jack, while he was alive, had included his wife in planning sessions about the future of the business, and if he had taken the time to explain to her what he wished her role to be, she would have known what was expected of her and what to leave alone. She could have learned this easily, even without business experience, and she could have helped to advance the wishes of the husband she loved.

Succession planning has to include a thorough airing of the responsibilities of ownership and control. When the spouse and the children are involved and informed, and there is family agreement over their individual roles, each one knows what to expect as a result of succession.

The benefits of *ownership*, such as dividends and the value of shares, are relatively easy to spell out in a succession agreement; the benefits of *control* are more varied and widespread, and their psychological impact is less easy to predict. Benefits which derive from control of a business include more than salaries, bonuses and fringe-benefit packages—they include all of the perks that accompany top management. I call salaries, bonuses and benefit packages *real* income; and I call perks and prestige benefits *psychic* income. In Ray Stilson's family, psychic income caused problems even though the succession plan had been agreed to by all of the family members.

Ray had three sons, each of whom shared ownership after Ray's retirement. His middle son, Howie, was the ablest and most interested in running the company, and he was made president. The other two sons had good jobs with other companies, and they agreed that Howie should run the company. He ran the company for about seven years, during which time the value of the company approximately doubled. By the end of that time, Howie was earning a $400,000 salary and drove a luxury company car. Twice each year, he took all of the salesmen on company-paid trips to Hawaii. He had a company-funded country club membership as well as a liberal expense account. Whenever all three sons and their families went out together, Howie picked up the company-paid tab. All of this was part of Howie's psychic income.

The other two sons saw that Howie was able to live in a lavish life style and they were not, even though they were all equal owners. They protested and asked for similar perks, which were not granted because they were unearned. Finally, in spite of their father's strong protests, lawsuits were filed. They have dragged on and there has been no conclusion except that a lot of money has been spent and the brothers have become perpetual adversaries.

My point here is that, in succession planning, there needs to be a good understanding of what it means to control a company—not only in terms of responsibilities and performance, but in terms of psychic as well as real income. Otherwise, envy and its resulting quarrels are frequent.

Deciding who will own and control the business in the future is often difficult for its founder. If the succession plan calls for the company to go to Mom, in trust, in order to avoid estate taxes, then Mom controls it and votes the stock. But if the sons and/or daughters are actually running the company, all kinds of personal issues can become enmeshed in company operations. In one instance, the wife of a client shouted at her son, "You didn't come over to see me this weekend—I'm going to fire you as president!" When a spouse has all the voting power and the persons managing the company have no ability to make changes, it is an almost certain recipe for problems.

Often, Dad, in choosing a successor, either doesn't want to hurt his children's feelings or he is caught in a web of perceived family expectations. After Hugh McDowell retired, it was assumed that the oldest of his two sons would take over the business, but Hugh refused to formalize it. Time after time I asked Hugh, "What's really bothering you about this issue?" Finally, he opened up and admitted he was afraid that his oldest son, Phillip, would fail, and that as a result, Hugh and his wife would lose their income. What Hugh really wanted was for his younger son, Rod, to be president of the company, but for several years the older son had been led to believe he would be given the nod.

I then said to Hugh, "Why don't we just ask your sons what *they* want?" At the next meeting of the Family Advisory Board, Rod said, "I don't need to be president. Let Phillip be president. I'm actually running the company now—anytime Phillip has a financial or administrative problem, he comes to me. I don't care what title you give Phillip or me, that doesn't matter to me."

Then it was Phillip's turn. He told us, "Look, I want to be president or chairman. My wife expects me to be president; all of my family expects me to be president. I don't want to be chief operating officer—Rod does that much better than I do."

In fact, the problem of who to choose as successor was no problem at all—except in their father's mind. In addition, to alleviate their father's anxiety about becoming impoverished, the sons agreed to borrow ten million dollars against company assets and give it to their parents as a retirement fund. Although this is an oversimplification of the issue, the main elements of a solution were resolved in a single evening. It was simply a matter of clearly communicating each persons's interests and needs.

It is important for you, the entrepreneur, to share your thoughts and feelings about succession with all other family members (and with others outside the family, if they are candidates for successor). You may temporarily disappoint and discourage those who aren't included in the list of potential successors, but, in fact, by communicating your thoughts, you will be doing each person a service. Moreover, you may be surprised by their reactions and by alternate ideas which they can contribute. As in the example of Rod and Phillip Mcdowell, siblings, and even cousins, often prefer to share responsibilities and control of the business. The top job is not the only job in the business. Other positions can be made very attractive with the inclusion of benefits and incentives. Also, because entrepreneurial families tend to have investment portfolios outside of the business, management of these nonbusiness assets can be a challenging and rewarding alternative to running the business.

Sometimes, when there is more than one competent successor, the best solution may be to split the business into separate divisions, or to buy another business in order to provide more leadership opportunities, or to simply follow the wishes of the children. This kind of openness brought about a good result in the family of

Elmo Budd. Elmo owned a large brewery, and his son and daughter were both competent but couldn't work together. Elmo was at a loss about what to do, so I suggested he ask his son and daughter to work out a possible solution by themselves. His son, Allen, wanted to take over the brewery; his daughter, Nattie, really wanted to start her own temporary-help agency, specializing in computer services. At a meeting of the Family Advisory Board, Nattie said, "My brother gets to run a company of his own—why shouldn't I be able to have my own company, too?" As a result of that meeting, Elmo and his children got together with their lawyers and accountants and figured out the best way to borrow enough to fund Nattie's business startup. Today, both the brewery and the computer service agency are doing well.

With clear communication and a measure of flexibility, it usually becomes evident that there are opportunities for everyone. The strongest reason for early communication about succession is that it will clear the air and prevent the backbiting and negative intrigue that flourish in a climate of secrecy. The strongest antidote to succession rivalry, among siblings or between family and nonfamily aspirants, is to let everyone who is involved know your intentions.

Sometimes, an heir is not competent but is chosen to be successor in spite of his limitations. This usually means that an existing business employee (or another family member) will take on the actual responsibility of running the company, and the heir will be a figurehead successor. This is workable if the actual nature of the arrangement is made absolutely clear to the heir and he agrees to it; if the actual nature of control is left vague so that the heir believes he is really in charge, it is a recipe for disaster. Also, the compensation level should reflect the real situation. If, for example, a vice-president is actually running the company, he should receive a salary and benefits that are commensurate with his actual responsibilities.

Having chosen one or more successors, it is important to test them until you are quite confident of their ability to do the job effectively, *before formally naming them.* Once one or more successors have been named, and those persons begin to take on appropriate responsibilities and gain a measure of control, it is very difficult to revoke your decision.

Looking at your own entrepreneurial skills, how long has it taken you to acquire them? Twenty years? Thirty years? How many years are you allowing your successor—your son or daughter or whoever it is going to be—to gain all of these skills? If you wait until you're seventy, your sharp, talented son or daughter isn't going to remain available that long. And if you're seventy, will you have the energy level (and the patience) to train him or her? It takes time to train someone properly, especially to acquire all of the varied skills needed by an entrepreneur; it may require ten to twenty years. Furthermore, your decision on one or more successors is going to have an impact on which way you take the company; how it will be structured and whether it will be retained or sold. Too many times, the family entrepreneur waits until he is seventy or more years old to make a decision on succession—a decision that should have been made when he was between forty and fifty.

Even the best-planned-for succession has to face the reality of dilution of ownership. Assume for the moment that you have four children. Though you have tried to involve all of them in the business, it's doubtful that all four of your grown-up children will be active, informed participants. And when your children each have four children of their own, are all sixteen grandchildren going to be interested and involved? No, that's not very likely or desirable.

The problem which arises is that, as ownership (and consequently, interest and involvement) is diluted, so is the family loyalty to maintain the company. The interests and needs of sixteen owners are so diverse that board meetings can become endless rounds of opposing views and bickering. Many family conflicts are caused by the differing interests of active owners—those who are directly involved with the business—and passive owners—those who are not involved (the majority). The active owners have a stake in the continuance of the company, while the passive owners are usually more interested in receiving payments for their share. If the founder's primary concern is for his heirs to maintain the company, this conflict can be avoided by creating a trust through which all of the heirs share the income from the company but only one or more trustees have decision-making authority.

The intact fortunes of most of the super-rich families in the U.S. can be traced to entrepreneurial founders whose succeeding generations retained stock while giving up incremental control. Sometimes, this happened by the eventual dilution of the stock, over time, through public offerings. Or the family chose to use professional managers while maintaining seats on the board to make sure that family interests were not ignored.

A succession decision obviously affects the company employees. If you decide to turn your company over to one or more of your grown-up children, or if your succession decision hasn't been made yet, how committed will your key executives be? If I am one of your executives, I know that if the company goes public or is sold, a new management team will probably be coming in. Why should I commit myself to staying with the company? The only way I will commit myself is if I know the company is going to remain intact and I have some guarantees—from you.

Retaining key executives; avoiding fights between heirs; allowing your chosen successor an adequate number of years to learn all the necessary skills; treating your grown-up children fairly as opposed to equally: these are a few of the many compelling reasons for squarely facing all of the succession issues now, while there is time and energy to do it right.

17 The Right Kind of Assistance

What is a family facilitator? The job is something like being a movie producer. A producer is part financial planner, part contract negotiator, part casting coordinator; and, to an extent, psychologist and mediator. The producer is the one who brings the whole package together and makes it work. Similarly, a facilitator wears several hats: estate planner, tax analyst, management consultant and family counselor. Like the producer, his task is to help make the whole production—the family—work together.

The movie producer must be careful not to define the story for the scriptwriter nor inhibit the vision and talent of the director. Similarly, an effective facilitator never determines family values and goals, and never usurps the authority of family members. He is there to help articulate the family's vision as *they* define it.

In estate planning, the common vision is to prepare assets for inheritance. But the facilitator broadens that definition and says that an estate plan insures that the children of clients are prepared to inherit wealth and use it wisely. In fact, across the whole spectrum of estate and succession planning, an effective facilitator introduces new ideas and ways of looking at problems so entirely new options can be considered by the family—options that were not previously available. One of the facilitator's goals is the establishment and continuation of family harmony, so that inheritors can work together instead of fighting each other and wasting money and energy in post-succession litigation.

The facilitator addresses the personal as well as the business and legal aspects of a family. In the process, he may ask the entrepreneur some tough questions, like: "Can you objectively evaluate the competence of each of your children?" Or "If you love your family, how can you justify spending so little time with them?" Or "Are you avoiding preparing for succession and, if so, what do you think are the real reasons for this?" The facilitator must raise and bring to the table gut-level issues, because they have a powerful impact on any plan that is going to be prepared.

These are all sensitive issues, and frequently, family members are so wrapped up in their patterns of relating that an objective guide is needed to resolve underlying conflicts. As that guide, the facilitator must be able to span all of the relevant issues and bring his experience to bear on everything from sibling rivalry to tax law. Thus the facilitator brings to his clients a unique blend of skills and experience. He does not replace traditional advisers, like lawyers and accountants; he integrates their advice into a comprehensive plan which is designed to implement the goals of individual family members, as well as the collective goals of the family as a team.

How do you find a competent and effective facilitator who is right for your family? Basically the same rules apply as for finding competent and effective lawyers, accountants, money managers and other advisers. First, I suggest you write out a job description of what you want accomplished and then set this out in an appropriate time frame. If you do not provide your advisers with clear guidelines and priorities, you will probably be wasting a lot of time and money, as your advisers attempt to guess what you really want from them. As with any other hiring, you should make as much use as possible of all of your personal contacts, to find out their opinions of, and experience with, your candidate(s).

When you are choosing advisers, it is important you choose people with some experience at your level of net worth. A lawyer, accountant or money manager who is only experienced with estates up to ten million dollars may not have the competence to deal with fifty million dollar estates; and the adviser who is experienced with fifty million dollar estates may not have the expertise to work with estates of several hundred million dollars or more. Each higher level is a different ball game, which requires experience at that level.

Another thing to look for in advisers is their ability to be team players. This is essential because much of their responsibility is to work with other advisers. I have seen too many occasions when an individual has exhibited initiative, creativity, independence and follow-through, but has simply not had the ability to coordinate his efforts with others.

In general, my staff and I counsel all of our clients to check out and personally talk to *all* listed references. It is amazing how often references are *not* checked, with the result of incompetent or inappropriate advisers being hired. I ask my clients to interview all candidates personally, and to get to know their personal values. Your feelings about working with a facilitator are very important. No matter how impressive his credentials, if you don't *like* dealing with him, pass him up and find someone you do like.

One of the roles of the facilitator may be to help find other advisers with whom all members of your family are comfortable. In the final analysis, mutual trust is the absolutely essential ingredient between you and your advisers, and your own intuitive sense will be your guide.

18 The Challenge of Relinquishing

Sometimes, it's very hard to give up control of a business or other asset, even when you know you should and you've given your word that you will. Arthur Britten recently went through this. Art has several broadloom mills near Atlanta. He has two very capable children—his son, Macon and his daughter, Deirdre—who were in their mid 30's when this lesson began playing itself out. Both of his children were anxious to take over more business responsibilities, and when I met with the family, Art said he thought that they would be ready to take over one of his companies in about five years. I asked Art, "Why the five years?" and he cited several skills that they needed to acquire, and some specific experience he felt they needed.

I encouraged Art to draw up a list of requirements and present it to his son and daughter; specific objectives they would have to meet before he would consider them ready. No time limits were placed on his children in meeting these requirements. Art made up the list, and he gave his word that he would turn one of his companies over to his son and daughter, once his conditions had been met.

With this agreement in hand, Macon and Deirdre worked very hard at learning what was necessary. To Art's surprise, instead of taking five years to meet his conditions, they did it in two years.

Faced with the reality of letting go of one of the four companies he had built single-handedly, Art started waffling and it wasn't clear that he was going to live up to his word.

Art went through some powerful emotions over this, and he realized how hard it was for him to let go of something he really valued. At one point I advised him, "Art, you've got to follow through on your commitment, or you'll lose your credibility with your children, and your relationship with them will really suffer. Is the company worth that?" Finally, he came through and he made Macon president and Deirdre CFO of his Dalton, Georgia mill. To his credit, Art left them alone to run it their way, giving advice only when it was requested. The first year of the children's management was unprofitable, but by the last quarter of the second year, they had turned it around and produced both strong growth and a healthy profit.

Actually, Art had a relatively easy time of it; he was still actively managing three carpet mills. When an entrepreneur tries to let go of a single business, much more is at stake, including a loss of identity. Often this letting go happens abruptly, because of illness or some other unplanned-for event. In these cases, there has been no preparation, and the entrepreneur doesn't have time to build a new self-image. Feeling lost and empty, he may (often subconsciously) sabotage his successor.

Harv Fremont did this when he retired from running his groundwater testing laboratory. Harv had been the key man at the helm for many years and, before he retired, he brought in a new CEO. He gave the new man full responsibility, but Harv knew, or sensed, that the expertise to run a laboratory that must consistently and accurately measure trace amounts of chemicals (to the parts per billion) in water, could not be learned without lengthy, on-the-job experience.

Sure enough, after the new CEO had been on the job for about nine months, the lab began making significant errors and was about to be decertified. Harv was able to come out of retirement and save the sinking ship. He was the hero—the unexpendable owner!

Withholding required knowledge or authority from a successor is a common and well-known phenomenon among retiring entrepreneurs. It occurs if the successor is brought in from the outside, is an employee of the company or even is a son or daughter of the owner. It's just hard to let go.

Another client, Bob Oliver, seemed more enlightened. He decided to retire at age fifty-eight from his foundry which produced precision turbine blades for rocket motors. Bob promoted his Vice-President for Marketing to the role of CEO. Then Bob and his wife spent the next six months traveling—something he'd never had time to do before.

When Bob walked into his old office, after being gone for six months, he was shocked to see that his pictures weren't on the wall behind his desk. His award plaques had been taken down. The whole office had been rearranged. Bob was outraged. He bellowed at his old friend, "How dare you take down my pictures! Who do you think you are? Because I named you president doesn't give you the right to re-do my office!"

The man who was the recipient of all this anger was so taken aback he couldn't speak. As far as he knew, Bob was retired and gone. He couldn't figure out why all the hostility was coming at him.

Later, Bob apologized to his president and confided to me that when he saw that his things had been removed, he was just devastated. He said it was one of the most painful times he could remember—the feeling of not being needed anymore.

There are many reasons why entrepreneurs hesitate, prolong, and even come back out of retirement. The reasons include loss of identity, lack of contact with close business acquaintances, sheer boredom and lack of confidence in successors ("What if my kids fail? What do my wife and I do for income?"). When a retirement date gets close, what I hear often is "Roy, I've been reconsidering," "Roy, I've just got a few things I want to tidy up," "Roy, I just need to get through this quarter." Underneath these casual rationalizations, the entrepreneur is frequently terrified.

There are several things we recommend our clients do to smooth the transition to retirement. For example, when Mary Petreska retired as CEO of a large construction subcontracting firm, she retained a small office and a modest, symbolic salary from the company. Mary shows up once or twice a month to help the company make use of her many personal contacts. She has her desk to go to, an active file of contacts, and old friends to see at the office. This arrangement is a win-win situation; the company makes use of Mary's knowledge and she still feels needed.

What we emphasize most to each of our clients is the importance of preparing ahead of time for retirement. Here are some of our suggestions.

- Plan a specific future date for retirement and stick to it as if it was inviolable.

- Maintain some minimal form of involvement with the business. In many cases, becoming a member of the Board, or Chairman of the Board, is an excellent way to broaden your perspective without having to be involved in day-to-day activities.

- If possible, arrange for necessary retirement income to come from outside the business, so your life style doesn't depend on your successor(s).

- Retain a physical office and a secretary to keep up your files and handle correspondence, etc.

- Plan ahead of retirement, with several non-business interests to keep you occupied. Consider involvement with philanthropy or make use of the prodigious knowledge you have acquired over the years by teaching (formally, at a college, or informally, through community groups).

- Be prepared for the possibility of a certain amount of temporary depression. This is a major change in your life, and it isn't always easy, in spite of preparation. Be aware that this may be a difficult re-orientation period, and seek professional help if it becomes overwhelming.

In Chapter 7, I presented a system of charting life values, called the Five Equities. In this system, I described a process for defining your values and your short- and long-term goals. Approaching retirement is the time to revaluate these values and goals; to see how far along you are to reaching them, and what are the next steps to bring them to fruition.

A lack of retirement planning usually creates problems with the entrepreneur's family, with employees and with the entrepreneur, himself. Lack of planning can also shorten the retiree's life. Actuarial studies by insurance companies typically show a brief life span for a retiree who does not remain physically or mentally involved.

Retirement can be a time of wonderful opportunities. For many entrepreneurs, who have spent much of their lives tending the business almost exclusively, retirement is a time to begin tending their total lives—something they have never before had the time, the energy or the money to do.

And lastly, timely retirement is an integral part of the process of preparing your grown-up children for inheritance; it gives them the opportunity and incentive to build on your efforts, while they are at their peak of performance and interest.

19 Choosing the High Road

In the play, *All My Sons*, by Arthur Miller, a manufacturer is caught up in an ethical dilemma. The time is World War II, and he has a contract to make precision parts for U.S. war planes. He is behind schedule and is facing strong pressure to meet his quota. But the latest batch of parts have come through with defects. This entrepreneur is generally honest and patriotic, but the pressure on him is intense. If he rejects the parts, he will lose the contract, he will sustain a huge loss and he will be discredited. If he ok's the parts, there is a chance that they will fail, leading to the possible loss of pilots and planes. The play is made more dramatic by the fact that the boss's own son is an Air Force pilot.

He decides to approve the parts and ship them. As the play leads to its conclusion, the man learns that his own son has been killed when his plane crashed, due to those defective parts. The man's role in shipping the defective parts is exposed, and his life collapses around him in ruin.

While the drama of this play is a relatively rare occurrence, over the years I have noticed a creeping tendency in our society to overlook the ethics of a situation in order to reap a short-term gain. This tendency is noticeable in some prominent business schools, where the prevailing ethos seems to be to maximize profit, *regardless of the consequences*. It's as though making money has become an end in itself.

There are many occasions when a short-term gain can be made by ignoring the ethics of the deal; and sometimes lean times make these gains very compelling. But as anyone who has been in business for a length of time knows, the "high road"—that is, the road of ethics, morality, integrity and generosity—is the only way to go which will insure long-term success.

My own personal opinion is that the world of commerce is not exempt from the spiritual laws that govern our lives. From my own experience, I am convinced that there are basic principles which impact upon the businessman or the manager of wealth. I have found, for example, that whatever your actions, they will often attract like actions back to you; if you are committed to taking advantage of people, the world will respond by providing you with ample opportunities to hurt yourself. If you go out of your way to help others, you, too, will receive help—often from unexpected sources.

There seems to be an organized system of energies in the world that respond not only to what we do but to what we think, as well. I believe the best way to harmonize with and make use of these energies is to follow your heart—follow your own sense of what is right, and make sure you are not hurting anyone else in the process.

I know I am not saying anything new here. If you are an experienced entrepreneur, you have, no doubt, been through many, many ethical and moral tests in your own life. This kind of experience is not something you learn in school—it comes from years of making tough choices and living with them. I call this kind of accumulated knowledge, "wisdom." My main purpose here is to encourage you to share your wisdom with your children.

In my own life, I know that my children are my greatest asset. Were they also my greatest headache? Yes, that too. Would I do it all over again if I had the chance? Yes, and I'd have more children, because they are the greatest achievement of my life. But most importantly, I would again make sure that I encourage my children to choose the High Road. If this single task is done well, most other things will fall into place. What more profound legacy could we possibly leave our children?

20 Completing the Process

Throughout this book I've emphasized that the process of preparing your children to inherit your wealth is not a quick fix. It isn't something that you can start tomorrow and finish next week. It requires a strong and continuing commitment from you and from your family.

Some of the questions I've raised are: What is your relationship with your children? How prepared are they to manage wealth? Will their inheritance provide them with opportunities to enhance their own lives and the lives of those around them, or will it be a destructive burden to them? Are you doing everything you can to promote their ethical, moral, social and financial development?

What do you want to do with your assets? Do you want to give them to your children, to charity, or will you, by default, give them to the government? If you have put together an estate distribution plan, will your business and other assets be transferred the way you want them to be—whether that transfer is to key employees, children, grandchildren or cousins? And will that transfer of assets be "fair?"

In making a commitment to this process, are you really willing to spend the time necessary to prepare your children? Are you willing to strike a reasonable balance between the time and energy devoted to business and the time and energy devoted to your family? And are you willing to share your values and skills with your children, and work toward building a family team?

In seeking the answers to these kinds of questions, I have made reference several times to the functions of a family facilitator. I've described how a facilitator can help to smooth family relationships, clarify goals and implement plans. But for the assistance of a family facilitator to be most effective, your active participation is essential. You must be willing to look at controversial, emotional or unspoken issues that exist within your family and which have a bearing on their future. Current and potential family conflicts have to be squarely faced and, to the extent possible, reconciled.

If you are willing to do these things, and if you can start using the many tools I've described in this book—communicating through a Family Advisory Board; forming a family bank and family partnerships; supporting business apprenticeships for your grown-up children and setting standards for their performance; learning to deal with advisers, to name a few—you will begin to develop confidence in this process.

Once you are fully committed to this process, you will gain a great deal of satisfaction as you watch your children's skills and judgment improve in such areas as risk-taking, money management, using advisers and working as a team. As the process continues, you will be more and more confident that your sons and daughters will use your assets responsibly, that they will mature into well-balanced individuals who understand how wealth is acquired and maintained, and the high standards of performance that are necessary to do this. In preparing your children to inherit your wealth, there are many diverse elements to remember. The following Summary Of Preparation Steps lists the basic necessary elements that need to be in place.

Summary Of Preparation Steps

1. My succession plan has been formulated, a date set and a replacement identified and trained.

2. I have a current will that has been reviewed in the last year.

3. My assets are structured for transfer to my heirs or to charities in the most efficient way possible.

4. My heirs are prepared to inherit and manage my wealth so it becomes a blessing and not a burden.

5. All legal agreements have been reviewed with my partners and/or shareholders during the last year and agreed to.

6. All of my adult children participated in the development of my estate plan.

7. The issue of fair vs. equal inheritance has been discussed within my family.

8. My children know and feel comfortable with my trusted advisers and key people.

9. I hold family board meetings at least yearly.

0. Any subject is open for discussion at these meetings. Money, my net worth and succession issues are examples of this.

11. My estate plan includes the minimization of estate and transfer taxes and maximizing the benefits to my heirs and to charity.

12. I have run a "fire drill" in regard to my estate planning, and everyone knows what to do and how to respond if I die unexpectedly.

13. The relationships among my family and extended family are excellent and my wealth will not create legal or emotional turmoil after I die.

14. Our family communicates openly about issues of disagreement, business practices and family relationships.

15. My life is balanced between family and business and I have interests other than business to bring balance to my life.

16. The *control* of my wealth and business vs. the *ownership* of them have been considered and discussed with my family.

17. My business Board of Directors includes outsiders for perspective and objectivity, and they know my family well.

18. My family can readily identify the five people in whose business and financial judgment I trust completely, and they feel comfortable asking their advice.

19. I have installed a process of educating my heirs to prepare them to inherit my business, wealth and values.

20. Our family values, as well as personal values, have been discussed openly within the family.

21. My business planning has included the successful management of the company during the transition time between my death and my successors' implementation of the succession process.

22. If I died suddenly, my wife would have no difficulty sustaining her current life style into the foreseeable future.

23. I have selected my retirement date, and everyone knows the date and who will take over.

Even after a succession plan and an estate distribution plan are in place, there are some on-going tasks. It's necessary to periodically update goals and plans, and to modify all relevant documents to reflect changes. For example, if a new grandchild arrives, it is easy amidst all of the excitement to forget to add that child's name to the will. I recommend to my clients that, semi-annually or at least annually, the Family Advisory Board, including all outside advisers, meet for a review of any necessary changes. This review meeting should be formally scheduled and attended by all family members.

With the processes I have described, I am really asking you to take all of the intelligence, energy, creativity and determination you have so successfully focused on your business and bring it to bear on the challenge of preparing your children and forging a family team.

It has been an extraordinary thing for me to watch and assist formerly tense, uncooperative, feuding families openly discuss their differences, and then proceed to tolerance, then mutual respect, and then reaffirmation of love for each other. I have watched the most intransigent sons and daughters, the most stubborn, narrow-minded fathers begin to actively help each other. And I've seen individual goals and family goals, for the first time, become complementary rather than remain antagonistic. Often, this process of forging a family team seems to yield more results in six months than therapy sessions may do in ten years.

As I'm sure you have gathered from this book, my staff and I feel strongly about strengthening the American Family. One of the things we believe to be of real value in accomplishing this is the creation of family missions.

The Family Mission

The breakdown of family unity is the most prevalent of the problems other members of my staff and I encounter. There are many reasons for this, including divorce, parents working in separate places, parents traveling much of the time, and children going to school long distances from home. Adding to this are the decreasing authority of traditional institutions and the loss of heroes. Family unity has suffered as a result of all of these. This is seen in the increasing number of intra-family legal battles which challenge the emotional as well as the economic survival of the family.

So the family as a unit is breaking down—emotionally, as well as economically. Many years ago, families would sit around the fire and listen to stories. These stories helped to sustain a sense of unity and belonging. Today, our children are involved in worthwhile activities such as athletic teams, dance classes and drama clubs. Parents are also involved—with business, social and charitable activities, all of which are worthy. But no one is creating the myths, stories and traditions that create and sustain family unity.

Just as any business needs long-term goals and a mission in order to succeed, so do families need reasons to build a future together. Over the years I have seen parents provide generously for their heirs, but what I have found missing is provision for how the children and grandchildren can act together to further common goals.

One of the tasks of my company is to encourage the creation of family missions, which respect both individuality and shared purpose. By creating family traditions, missions and goals, family diversity becomes a strength and a joy, and family members share a bond that is strengthened by communication, trust and love. No matter how dysfunctional a family initially is, I have never seen the re-emergence of the family as a unit fail if all members are committed to this process.

I hope you have found the information I have presented useful, and that you, too, will take up the challenge of preparing your family to manage your wealth. I know each of you will gain from the experience, and that your family will continue to grow in common purpose.

Appendix A
Concerns and Actions

A listing of typical client concerns and corresponding actions taken by The Williams Group to address these concerns.

"I AM CONCERNED ABOUT THE LACK OF TRUST AND COOPERATION IN MY FAMILY AT PRESENT."

Concerns	Actions
I see resentment and resignation in my family, and I don't like it.	We will lead one session on moods, and offer new working definitions for what they are, how they affect your family, and how to shift them. We will discuss how moods may become self-fulfilling prophecies in family relationships.
How do I deal with "pillow talk," back-biting and family resentments?	We will offer guidance, and at the end of the first year, your heirs will report that they trust each other—and you—more than they did at the start of the year; and specifically that they trust you in one area of your relationship where they had a lack of trust before.

Concerns	Actions
I'm concerned about my in-laws' motivations. My family and our in-laws don't have much in common.	We will ask all family members to give a report on what is important in their lives. We will guide family members in becoming better observers of what *all* family members have in common, and how this can bring the immediate family and in-laws together in shared goals and action.
My concerns are not being addressed by my family. They say I don't understand them. How can we communicate better?	We will offer a new working definition of good communication. We will lead at least two sessions on how you know when good communication has taken place and how to produce it. We will use a family member's existing interpretation of good communication, and then ours, for at least two situations that person chooses as being particularly important in his or her life. As a result, they will see new possibilities for better communication.
There are a lot of important and nagging issues our family just doesn't talk about, but I know they're there.	We will participate in up to four family meetings a year, and will assist the family member who is the chairman of each meeting in setting up and prioritizing an agenda. We will poll each family member for agenda items and, if they are unable or unwilling to bring up a certain topic, we will do it and coach the family on how to discuss it beneficially.

"I AM CONCERNED THAT MY CHILDREN WILL BE HARMED RATHER THAN HELPED BY THEIR INHERITANCE."

Concerns

I see my wealth becoming a burden to my spouse and heirs.

Actions

We will set up investments, involving less than 10% of the family's net worth, that will give your heirs experience in managing assets of the type in your estate. We will assist you in choosing assets, and we will coach your family and have them report on their progress at least quarterly. We will introduce your family to the responsibilities of having a family "financial organization." We will interview each family member to see which responsibilities, if any, they see themselves managing. By the end of the second year of our contract, your family will report confidence in handling the family's affairs in the event of your demise.

I am concerned that my heirs' self-images are based on materialistic values.

We will use a worksheet which will reveal the values of yourself and your family, and we will lead a discussion on the purpose of wealth. You and your family will develop an outline of a family mission statement which incorporates and supports individual and family values and goals.

Concerns	Actions
I've always treated my children equally, but will that kind of estate plan fit my heirs' circumstances or skills?	By the end of the third family meeting, you and your family will have a plan that allows you or a trustee discretion to distribute according to needs and circumstances that you choose.
I want my wealth to be an incentive for my heirs to become responsible.	Within the first year of our contract, you will form a partnership or joint venture with at least two family members, including a parent, for the purpose of buying and managing an investment. This investment will be chosen by your heirs after consulting with both you and us. We will introduce one of your children to a due diligence process, and he or she will use that to find and interview an attorney who is competent, by our standards, in partnerships and taxation. Another son or daughter will take a written list of objectives to this attorney, and manage the development of a partnership agreement, its review, approval and signing by all partners.

"I AM CONCERNED THAT MY HEIR'S INHERITANCE WILL DRIVE THEM APART RATHER THAN BRING THEM CLOSER TOGETHER."

Concerns

I want our family's wealth to be "glue" and not "dynamite."

I don't want my wealth to destroy my heirs' marriages.

I am concerned that after I die, my heirs will fight with each other.

Actions

We will introduce at least three proven ways to bring your family together, at least two of which you are not now doing. We will review each of these methods and advise you on which ones will work best for your family—and the reasons for that assessment—in writing, before the end of the first year. After you and your family decide which to use, we will prepare a written offer for coaching your family in the implementation of this plan.

In-laws and their spouses will be interviewed to identify their concerns and goals. In-laws will be invited to all family meetings. We will encourage each couple in developing their own mission statement for the family. We will offer coaching on how wealth affects self-esteem and marriages, and what possibilities, both positive and negative, it brings to a marriage.

We will present the economics of your estate plan to your family, and they will report that your estate planning team has seriously considered all of their stated concerns.

"I AM CONCERNED THAT OUR FAMILY WEALTH WILL DISSIPATE RATHER THAN BE PRESERVED."

Concerns

Actions

I am concerned the government is going to take more than half of my estate.

We will show you how to reduce your estate tax cost to less than 20%.

I am concerned that my heirs do not have any interest in managing my business and/or wealth.

With our supervision, at least one of your children will report to the family on your business by the end of the first year of our contract. After this, all of your children will report a clearer understanding of your business which will show them new possibilities that the business can offer them.

I am concerned that my heirs are not now prepared to manage my assets.

We will introduce the fundamental distinctions between the skills needed in creating wealth versus preserving wealth. We will introduce due diligence processes for investments that are of interest to your heirs, including real estate, venture capital and securities. We will provide sessions that show them what investment alternatives are available to them.

Your family will establish an investment partnership by the end of the first year of our contract. This partnership will require that one or more of your children hire and work with an attorney to establish the partnership.

Concerns

Actions

We will coach them through a due diligence process for hiring a money manager for the family, and will give them specific guidance on this process. By the end of the year, they will have hired a money manager. After the manager is hired, we, together with your family, will have at least two interviews with the manager, and we will offer our assessment of the manager's performance at least twice a year.

Each family member, either alone or in partnership, will actively participate in a money management project of his or her choosing. By the end of the first year of our contract, each of your children will have produced a report on what they believe their competences, or incompetences, are in managing the asset in this partnership.

By the end of the second year, each of your children will have a will which embodies a plan of distribution that each has produced.

By the end of the second year, each of your children will have met with their accountant (and may have to select one for themselves) and will be able to speak about what each entry on their federal tax form means.

By the end of the second year, you and your heirs will demonstrate new skills that you,

Concerns	Actions
	we and they say show prudence. They will say that they are confident they can choose an appropriate team to manage the family's wealth.

"I AM CONCERNED THAT OUR FAMILY ASSETS HAVE BECOME TOO COMPLICATED FOR ME OR MY CHILDREN TO CONTROL."

Concerns	Actions
All these new laws and restrictions are continually taking away my choices.	We'll show you how the new laws are still voluntary, and we will present you with at least three possible strategies from which you can choose.
I am concerned that my heirs will feel and act powerless when they are confronted with the complexities of managing my estate.	You heirs will observe (and possibly participate in) the planning process, and will be told why certain decisions were made. Your lawyer and accountant will be invited to a family meeting to introduce themselves and to tell your heirs in simple terms what the estate plan means for them. Your heirs will be told by us what rights and control they have over the estate, and choices they have for delegating management of the estate if they feel it is necessary.

Concerns

I just don't know if my plans will really work. Sometimes, I throw up my hands and say, "Let the kids and the lawyers worry about it."

Actions

We will supervise a "fire drill" where your children and your lawyers *do* worry about it, while you observe. The fire drill begins with "Dad's dead—who's got the will?" We will make a checklist of what went well and what didn't. Then we will advise you on what can be done to correct deficiencies.

"I AM CONCERNED THAT OUR FAMILY'S VALUES MAY NOT BE PRESERVED EVEN THOUGH OUR WEALTH IS."

Concerns

How do I preserve our family's values as well as our wealth?

Actions

We will provide sample questions from which you can outline a family mission statement. We will coach you, as you request, throughout the process of developing a mission statement, for up to ten hours of our time, at which point we will make a proposal for future work. During one of the first two family meetings, we will lead a session on one or more ways of identifying and clarifying you and your family members' values. We will request written responses to questions that will reveal concerns in many areas of life. At certain points in this process, we will suggest actions family members can take to act on their values together.

Appendix B
Succession
Instruments

The Buy/Sell Agreement

The Buy/Sell Agreement is a means for enabling one or more owners of an asset (a company, investment portfolio, property, etc.) to sell their shares to the remaining owners at a future date, in accordance with prearranged terms. It is a legal document whose purpose is to allow part owners to sell their interest without destroying the asset and without the need for litigation.

For example, in a partnership, if one partner should die, the surviving partner(s) can agree in advance to buy the business from the heirs of the deceased partner, at a predetermined price. Funding for this buy-out might be needed for several reasons. The business may have to continue paying the deceased partner's salary to his estate and, at the same time, hire and pay another manager to take his place; or there may be an estate tax liability due to the event of a death; or the firm's credit line may be discontinued in the event of a partner's death. Because the event of a death creates a liability, one of the best ways to provide for it is through life insurance, where that same event also creates a solution. Regardless of what type of funding vehicle is used, an essential part of a buy/sell agreement is that the funding for a possible future sale is in place. This agreement involves preparing several projections. For example, what will the value of the business be in the future? This is usually determined by assuming a certain percentage for inflation plus a certain percentage for growth; or, it can be determined by current company value, sales, etc.

The most critical part of the Funded Buy/Sell Agreement is determining the costs of the funding. Someone must run the actual numbers to come up with a basis for showing a present value cost of alternate funding vehicles.

Charitable Foundations

There are basically two kinds of charitable organizations: public charities which either have a broad base of public support or actively support other public charities; and private foundations, which are usually controlled and supported by a single source, such as an individual donor, a family or a company.

Private foundations are further divided into operating foundations and nonoperating foundations. Private nonoperating foundations basically give money to other charitable organizations. In contrast, private operating foundations support programs and activities operated by the foundations themselves. Accordingly, a private operating foundation is able to support virtually any type of charitable activity in which it is actively involved and as long as it is consistent with the foundation's purpose. This type of foundation may also carry over excess income into future years for foundation activities.

A private operating foundation requires more extensive planning in its structure and activities in order to obtain approval from the IRS as a tax exempt organization, but the results are worth the effort. Donations to private operating foundations receive preferential tax treatment compared to donations to nonoperating foundations. Most charitable foundations in the United States are nonoperating foundations, not because of the difficulties involved with the IRS approval, but simply because many lawyers and tax accountants are unaware of operating foundations. Unless specifically qualified as operating foundations, all private foundations are nonoperating foundations by default.

Creating a charitable foundation satisfies several needs at the same time. First of all, it may avoid paying estate taxes upon the death of the father or mother or both (depending on how the estate is set up) by removing assets from the estate prior to death, with a corresponding charitable deduction. When the foundation is set up while dad and mom are still alive, they can get personal satisfaction and recognition from becoming involved with a university, hospital, etc., and at the same time, obtain some current income tax deductions. In addition, by involving their children with the foundation, parents can enable them to gain operating experience and monitor their performance. Finally, if an operating foundation is established, the family can engage in charitable activities created and managed by the foundation and family members can continue operations after the death of the parents.

For example, if you transfer assets to a qualifying foundation, any amount given to such a foundation will not be taxable at your death, and gift taxes can be avoided as well, even on property with capital gains, with proper planning and observance of the tax rules.

As members of the board, the adult children will help determine how the money is distributed. If the foundation is a nonoperating foundation, they will have to make sure that the foundation gives away all of its income every year.

By participating in the operation of a foundation, adult children learn not just how to give away money, but how to do it responsibly. In addition to giving away money, they are also giving of their time and energy. For the adult children, it is a hands-on course in money-management and assessing and doing something about social needs. If an operating foundation is created, the adult children can also gain firsthand knowledge of charitable and management activity through creating and supervising foundation programs.

The Will Summary

Because of their extensive legalese, wills are usually not readily understood by the layperson who wants a quick read. Many find it hard to remember the precise stipulations of a will years after it has been drawn up. For these reasons, I recommend my clients have their lawyer prepare a one-page, informal summary of the will that is not a legal part of it but which is simply folded inside of the will and which accompanies it. This summary of the will should state, in simple language, an outline of the client's goals and what the will accomplishes. The purpose of the will summary is to help a client remember what he or she was trying to accomplish with a particular will. If a client's goals have changed since the will was drawn up, and the will needs updating, the summary makes this clear. The need to change a will because of additional children, grandchildren and in-laws, or changes in a client's values, can be identified and the client's lawyer contacted for an update, codicil or new will. The will summary should be updated each time the will is changed.

Appendix C
Suggested
Additional Reading

Fathers—Not Managers—Know Best, Sue Shellenbarger, Wall Street Journal, September 12, 1991

Servant Leadership, Robert K. Greenleaf, Paulist Press, Ramsey, NJ, 1977

Unconditional Love, John Powell, Tabor Publishing, Allen, TX, 1978

Chop Wood, Carry Water, Rick Fields, Peggy Taylor, Rex Weyler and Rick Ingrasci, St. Martin's Press, New York, 1984

Beyond Survival, Leon Danco, University Press, Cleveland, 1975

Creating Effective Boards, John S. Ward, Jossey-Bass, Inc., San Francisco, 1991

Family Business Review, Journal of the Family Firm Institute, Jossey-Bass, Inc., San Francisco

Family Foundations At Work, Kelin E. Gersick, John A. Davis, Kevin Seymour, a research report of the California School of Professional Psychology, Whitman Institute, San Francisco 1990

Flow—The Psychology Of Optimal Experience, Mihaly Csikszentmihalyi, Harper Perennials, New York, 1990

Love and Profit, James A. Autry, Morrow, New York, 1991